DEEP, HEAVY STUFF

DON AKE

Karla,
Read + Live Well!

Don Ake

Although many of these essays have been modified significantly for publication, they were originally published on the blog "Deep, Heavy Stuff" (deepheavystuff.blogspot.com) between January 2020 and February 2022.

ALSO BY DON AKE

Just Make Me a Sammich!

Will There Be Free Appetizers?

Turkey Terror At My Door!

DON'S BLOGS:

Ake's Pains (akespains.blogspot.com)

Deep, Heavy Stuff
(deepheavystuff.blogspot.com)

TABLE OF CONTENTS

INTRODUCTION

Don Ake is a very good friend of mine. And he shouldn't be.

After all, I am nowhere near the target audience for his infamous humor blog, *Ake's Pains*, detailing the misadventures and memoirs of a middle-aged man*.

On the contrary: At first glance, I might appear to be someone hellbent on getting *Ake's Pains* "canceled". As of the time of this writing, I am an individual in my late twenties with (to quote an *Ake's Pains* post on the subject) "a mouse in my pocket"—a term which I wholeheartedly embrace not only because I'm such a good sport but also because it is an absolutely adorable mental image. Along with being an editor, I am also a fiction author, mainly focusing on horror, fantasy, and sci-fi, and I work in IT. I am married but have no children, as my animals are more than enough for now. My birth year straddles the line between "millennial" and—the new generational scapegoat—"zoomer".

It's mainly for this reason that I kept quiet about having edited *Turkey Terror At My Door!*, the third *Ake's Pains* essay book, published by Project 89 Media in 2020. I (somewhat cheekily, I'll admit) wanted to preserve its authenticity, not wanting to perform the equivalent of admitting that your favorite Mexican restaurant is actually run by a bunch of white people who think they're making you "qway-suh-dilluhs".

So why am I telling you all this?

A common theme throughout *Deep, Heavy Stuff* is unity. All of us working together because—contrary to what the news and pop culture try to tell us—we're all on the same team. The sooner we realize that about ourselves and each other, the sooner we can make the world—or simply our world—a better place. And what better way to get this message across than hearing from one of the last people anyone would expect to even read, much less enjoy and try to keep up with, *Ake's Pains?*

I've known Don since 2017. We met at an author fair soon after I released my first book, *questionMark*, and he invited me to join the Write Stuff Authors' Group of Canton, Ohio.

I distinctly remember one of the first group meetings my husband and I went to. It was around February of 2018, and Don had brought in an early draft of "A Tribute to Midnight, Part 3: One Last Look" for some last-minute critiques before it was posted to *Ake's Pains*. The essay—a rare, non-humorous piece—was a reflection about the death of Don's first and only dog, as well as about how amazing dogs truly are. This hit home for me because a few weeks earlier, we had unexpectedly lost our own elderly dog, as a trip to the vet for what we thought was a manageable issue had turned into a grim diagnosis and a final goodbye.

I'd told Don this, and we discussed it for a while. I don't remember exactly what we said, but that day—despite

our difference in age, interests, and life experiences—
we truly became friends.

Another reason I bring all this up is that while *Ake's Pains* can only be truly appreciated by people born in a certain time and place, *Deep, Heavy Stuff* is universal. I can give this book to almost anyone, regardless of how old they are or where in the world they're from, and they will no doubt learn something valuable from it.

And I know this because I read it.

I hope you enjoy reading this book as much as I enjoyed working on it.

— Faryl

AUTHOR'S THOUGHTS

The *Deep, Heavy Stuff* blog idea was born at a Need to Breathe concert in February 2019. As I listened to the band present truth as truth, with no added conditions, I became convicted to do the same thing with my writings. This meant making a radical departure from my familiar humor writing. Humor writing is extremely easy for me. Writing about the serious issues of life is enormously more difficult.

It took almost a year of planning to develop the concept. In October of that year, I had a conversation with my friend "Ski" about what to name the blog. We couldn't come up with a name that we both liked.

Out of frustration, he asked, "What is this thing about again?"

I thought for a second and then replied, just as frustrated, "It's a bunch of deep, heavy stuff."

Sometimes you need to get frustrated to do your best work.

The blog debuted in January 2020, right before the pandemic hit. I didn't think the pandemic impacted my writing much until I edited this book. However, the essays truly reflect the stress, pain, and fear I was experiencing during this time. In this way, it indirectly serves as a journal of the trauma of 2020-2021.

The book contains some very personal essays. Several of these stories, I never wanted to tell. They are much too personal and much too painful. For instance, Chapter 3 entails me describing in intimate detail the worst day of my life. To do this, I had to relive that day and face it again and again throughout the editing process. There is another incident in that chapter that I wasn't comfortable describing until first sharing it with a pastor.

But even so, the book is not about me. It's only about you and how your life may be enriched by these words.

My hope is that these words will impact you in some meaningful way and they will change how you think about, and ultimately do life. Please enjoy—and grow.

A Few More Notes

If you are reading this many years from now, this book was written during the COVID-19 pandemic of 2020-2021. Hopefully, there will be no future pandemics, making this whole statement moot.

Finally, you can't write a book about deep, heavy stuff without dealing with issues of faith. Naturally, my perspective on life and truth reflects my personal faith. However, I have taken great care to present the contents as to be palatable to people of all faiths and religions. This includes people of limited or no stated faith. In that vein, I have not used traditional jargon, names, or titles so that you may read the text calmly and intently. Of course, all readers will disagree with some statements I make. This is a natural by-product of discussing deep, heavy issues, which are difficult to discuss and agree upon. I believe truth is truth, no matter the source. So, please join me in this dive into the deep, heavy stuff of life.

No matter who you are, where you're from, or what you believe, I thank you for reading this book, and I wish you peace.

PART I
REMEMBERING WHAT'S IMPORTANT IN LIFE

CHAPTER 1:
THE JOY OF GIVING

Giving is a delicate subject: It involves reducing your resources for the benefit of others. And since our money decisions are so personal, it is easy to get defensive or agitated when this subject is discussed. That makes it deep, heavy stuff.

But relax, I'm not going to tell you how to give, how much to give, or who to give to. Most importantly, I will not make you feel guilty for your choices. Giving out of guilt produces many negative emotions, much like being stolen from. There is a joy in giving, which I'm attempting to communicate.

This chapter is my personal journey on the concept of giving. I will share some intimate details that I would've rather not divulged, but they are essential to the narrative and will explain my actions. I do not intend to present myself as someone special; I suppose I have failed in this area more times than I realize.

I profess that every word in this narrative is accurate to the best of my recollection. It would be more impressive if I could remember more specific details. However, I have also withheld some information that is too personal and not absolutely necessary to understand the narrative. But the purpose here is not to impress you. My aim is to get you to discover the joy of giving, not the burden—to focus on the good, not the guilt. And then to put your faith or beliefs into action.

I realize this is a difficult issue for many people. I take the words of THE MAN on this subject as a command, not a suggestion. I do realize religious hucksters have exploited this concept to become rich and live in mansions, and I figure they will have to answer for their actions one day. For me, I'll just follow the command—and receive the promise.

GIVE, AND IT WILL BE GIVEN TO YOU

"Give, and it will be given to you."
This is a universal truth, espoused by most major religions. The idea is that if we do good and help others, the cosmos will ultimately pay us back in kind.

I guess religion does get involved in this because much of religion is about getting us to do what we don't want to do. What we know we should do but ultimately don't. However, giving is odd because we feel better when we do it. Not because it abstains us from guilt, but because it provides satisfaction, even joy in the process. There could even be evolutionary forces in play: "Let's not kill Grog because he shares his extra beast with us."

IS LIFE FAIR?

However, the "given to you" notion of this statement is more complex. The concept that "life is fair" somehow naturally lives deep within us, and even though we know that life is not fair—sometimes cruelly unfair—it still makes us feel better if we think things do even out in the end. We want life to be fair. We need to view life as fair. It's a white lie we tell ourselves so we can treat others with kindness and sleep soundly each night.

Religion introduces rules for giving because religion is big on rules, and if you tell people they should give, then you'd better include rules for giving, or else the people will either run off and start giving stupidly or, worse yet, give nothing at all. The number of rules exemplifies how important giving is to these religions. Of course, most organized religions rely on their adherents to give money to fund their own operations. This is acceptable up to a point, with Jim Bakker being the poster child for abusing the concept.

THE RICH HAVE ALWAYS BENT THE RULES

When THE MAN walked this earth, the rich and pious had written many rules about how a "holy" person should give his resources. Of course, like our tax laws today, the rules favored the rich because the rich wrote the rules.

The rich people used these rules to abuse the poor people psychologically and spiritually. The poor felt ashamed and frustrated because they could not meet the stringent requirements. Many of them may have stopped giving altogether because it was too demanding. However, it can be assumed the laws enabled the rich to avoid paying "their fair share" and provided some loopholes.

And to set things right and correct the misconceptions of this complex morass, THE MAN proclaims this simple edict:

Give, and it will be given to you. A good measure, pressed down, shaken together, running over, will be put into your lap; for the measure you give will be the measure you get back. *

There's a lot in that short statement. So let's unpack it.

GIVE

THE MAN brings the wisdom to set things right into this ugly, deceitful, complicated mess. Strangely, He does not go into a complex discussion about why all the invented rules are wrong. That would take much too long, would get into the tall weeds, and bore the common man to death. Plus, it would only make the issue more perplexing and confusing. However, He also does not rebuke the common people, the people who give too little, or those giving nothing at all. He does not launch into a lengthy sermon on the proper attitude towards giving—the people already know that and are well aware they are failing to comply.

No, THE MAN utters a simple one-word command: GIVE. He doesn't say when to give, how much to give, who to give to—just GIVE. So forget the rules, forget the complications, forget the excuses—just GIVE. It can't be plainer than that. If you want brilliance, there it is. You take down the rule-writers and challenge the actions of the rule-ignorers with just one word.

AND IT WILL BE GIVEN TO YOU

And there it is! Life *is* fair, and if you give to others, someday, the cosmos will pay back the favor, and you will be rewarded for your generosity. Even Steven! Karma! Payback!

Yes, here, THE MAN delivers the same message as most of the great gurus, deities, philosophers, and prophets throughout history. However, there is one huge difference. It's right there in those seven words, but we'll come back to that in a moment.

If THE MAN had stopped here, the statement would have been universally accepted and consistent with natural beliefs, but He did not. He kicked it up a notch. He continues:

GOOD MEASURE, PRESSED DOWN, SHAKEN TOGETHER, RUNNING OVER, WILL BE PUT INTO YOUR LAP. FOR THE MEASURE YOU GIVE WILL BE THE MEASURE YOU GET BACK.

In those times when you bought grain, most vendors would pour the grain to the top of your vessel and send you on your way. But the sellers who provided the most value would pour the grain in the container, press it down, shake it together to condense it, and then repeat the process until the grain was tightly packed and you received the maximum amount. Of course, people enjoyed getting the most shakes for their shekels.

So what THE MAN is saying here is that you will get more than a fair return on your giving.

And then He lifts the bar. He pumps it up. He raises the roof. After your vessel contains the maximum payback, *more* grain is going to be poured on top. So much that you can't contain it, so much that it overflows and spills over into your lap.

What THE MAN is proposing: Give, and you will receive back more than you give. So much more, it will overflow.

And this happens not by luck, or chance, or karma, etc. It is *deliberate*. Because the other difference in THE MAN's statement is: "and it will be GIVEN to you". If it is given, then there must be a "giver". THE MAN is saying that THE CREATOR will purposefully and generously give back to you *purposefully* and *generously*.

This is far beyond the teachings of other religions and philosophers. THE MAN has truly raised the standard. It's what separates the God from the gods.

Of course, on the surface, it appears the message is that if you want to get rich, just give stuff away to people. Or maybe, just give *me* your money, and you'll get more money back—a spiritual Ponzi scheme, as it were. And many religious hucksters on television have indeed perverted this teaching to become rich over the years.

But that is not what THE MAN is laying down. You do not give to get. You do not give so that you can benefit. It must be evaluated in the total teaching in THE BOOK about giving. The most important aspect is attitude. What is your attitude about giving to others?

If you give just to get back, you fail. If you give out of obligation, by following some rule, you fail. If you give, but feel regret, you also fail. It's all about the attitude. It's all about being able to help your fellow man by sharing your resources and expecting nothing in return.

THE MAN delivers this message to people who were failing at giving and knew it. They were confused by His response and must have considered it unrealistic and bizarre. But 2000 years later, it is still just as strange. It is difficult to explain, and difficult for His adherents to defend.

It appears to be a crazy, unbelievable statement... or is it?

* Luke 6:38

A LIFE-CHANGING EVENT

Most life-changing events are prominent occurrences, evident to the people around you. They happen externally but impact you internally. Then, there are those subtle, quiet rumblings, oblivious to everyone but you, that impact from the inside out.

It was the first week of December 1987. I had returned home from a mentally exhausting workday. Within minutes, my wife had delivered the following news:

- The refrigerator, which had been making strange noises, would need a major repair.
- The VCR[1], which doubled as our video camera, had stopped working and would need to be fixed before Christmas.

Footnotes for younger readers:

1. Video Cassette Recorder. It recorded television shows onto videotape. Mine was an expensive model where the part containing the tape detached. A separate camera plugged into it to record home movies.

- My master's thesis[2], which my wife had been typing into our first ever PC, had vanished from the 5 ¼" floppy disk[3].

Money was tight since my wife was at home, raising our young, mildly special-needs daughter. Two costly repairs would put a considerable dent in the Christmas budget. And it would take weeks for the thesis to be retyped, putting me way behind schedule for the submission deadline.

If these events had been spaced out just a few days, they still would have stung, but the impact would have been more easily absorbed. But everything hitting all at once was more than my psyche could take that evening.

I could not calm down. I kept rolling each of these events around in my head like a closed-loop horror film that I could not turn off. After dinner and putting my daughter to bed, I plopped down on the couch and turned on the television, hoping that would provide a much-needed escape from my worries. But I couldn't even concentrate on the program because it was being usurped by the one running through my brain:

---

2. This was a full MBA which took four years to complete going part-time. A thesis was not required, but I choose to do one through independent study because I enjoy researching and writing.

3. The first floppy disks were flimsy and had to be handled with care. You had to insert them into a "floppy drive" each time you started up the computer, and then, you saved your file on another floppy disk. The only way to "backup" your data was to save the same data on two disks, which you almost never did.

Refrigerator bill ... VCR bill ... Lost thesis ... Refrigerator bill ... VCR bill ... Lost thesis ...

I couldn't stop the loop while awake, so I decided to go to bed, even though it was just past 8:30. Except for illness, this was the earliest bedtime in my adult life. However, I am not the least bit tired. I'm wide awake, lying there in the dark, staring at the ceiling.

I was in quiet solitude. In our busy lives, we are never in quiet solitude, but it takes this condition for us to hear THE CREATOR speak: no light, no sound, just dark silence. It makes you wonder if monks actually have the secret to life. By extracting yourself from the noise, distractions, and pressures, you can achieve more happiness. I'll bet the monks' communication with THE CREATOR is much better than mine and yours. Let that sink in for a moment.

I was in distress. It was quiet, it was dark. So, naturally, I reached out to THE CREATOR for help in my plight. And I learned something important: THE CREATOR doesn't respond well when you offer up whiny complaints about your first-world problems.

First, there was the strong rebuke. *"You're actually complaining because your fancy, expensive VCR is broken?"*

Okay, when you put it *that* way, I guess that it is rather petty. Let's forget I even brought it up.

But it was too late.

Next came the revelation. I was told to imagine an expectant child running down the steps on Christmas morning, only to encounter just a Christmas tree with no presents underneath it (This is a powerful image—if you don't believe me, quick, imagine it yourself right now).

And this hit me where it hurts because I am an only child, which meant on Christmas morning, every single gift under that tree was mine, all mine. And better still, I was an only child of an only child, which meant every present under Grandma's tree was also mine (Gee, and you wonder why I love Christmas so much!).

But the image of that kid with no presents ravaged me. It tore open my soul, and I was hemorrhaging spiritual blood. "Yes, that's an awful scene, but what can *I* do about this?" I wondered.

Then came the command: My church had announced the previous Sunday they were collecting money to buy watches (apparently someone had an excess supply) to give to underprivileged kids as Christmas gifts. I immediately dismissed it as something I wouldn't bother with.

But now, the instruction was to donate $100 to this project. You cannot be serious. Oh, no! Absolutely not! I've got to pay for the refrigerator. I've got to pay for the VCR. I've got to pay for Christmas. No! There is no money left for any watches. Okay? Oh, *not* okay? Not okay at all. $100? Really? Okay, really ...

So that Sunday, I wrote a check for $100 for watches for Christmas gifts for some kids I didn't know and would never meet. And it did feel good to know none of *those* kids would go "giftless" this year.

The credit card took a hit, but the refrigerator got fixed. The VCR got fixed. And Christmas got fully paid for. It took my friend Fred, one of the early computer whizzes, all of five minutes to find where my thesis was hiding on that tricky floppy disk. And life was once again good. Christmas 1987 turned out great, and life went merrily along.

That discussion with THE CREATOR, in that solitude, changed my life. No, there was no audible voice, but the communication was crystal clear. So clear that I can recall it 34 years later. Yes, sometimes, life-changing events happen quietly inside you, but this started a fire which keeps on burning today.

FOR ME, IT'S HARDER TO RECEIVE THAN TO GIVE

For the measure you give will be the measure you get back.

The real test as to whether someone really has had a conviction, conversion, or life-changing event is not what they say—or, in this case, write—it's what they do as a result. You can say anything—claim anything—but does your behavior change?

You can dismiss or explain away my "Christmas conviction" if you wish, but my behavior most certainly changed. A few days after that "discussion", I wrote that check for $100. But the change didn't stop after that single check. That image of the kid with no Christmas presents had been burned into my brain.

As a result, donations were made to various Christmas gift drives in 1988, 1989, 1990, and 1991. But there would be no check written in 1992. In October, I had been downsized from my job, a casualty of the economic recession. Now, I found myself on the other side: not providing help but needing help.

But I was much too proud to ask for or even receive help. I would have to be near death before I'd agree to receive aid from anybody. However, soon after the job loss, THE CREATOR spoke to me again. I was told that soon, people would be giving me aid. When they did, I was to accept it all and say, "Thank you".

You see, when you reject the help of others, you prevent them from following THE MAN's "GIVE" command. If you don't accept the gift, you prevent that person from receiving the blessing of giving the gift. That's wrong for you to do; some would even call it a sin.

And yet, I only actually asked two people for help the entire time. More troubling than losing my income was losing my health insurance. My oldest daughter (I had two daughters now) had a seizure disorder. The seizures would occur at random times and, depending on the severity, could produce a $20,000 hospital bill. Therefore, going without insurance was not an option, and a cheap policy wouldn't suffice. I would have to find a way to make the expensive COBRA payments.

I was given the name of a social service worker who a friend thought could help me with this expense. I lived in a different county than the agency, so I assumed they could not help me. I started the conversation with the social worker by apologizing for even calling. But after telling her where I worked, she asked me what county my former company resided in. Oh, it seems the funding covers both people who live in that county and work there. Then she instantly approved me for two months of COBRA payments.

My mother helped me with the other two payments I ended up needing. But I'm not sure asking your mother for help even counts since I'd been doing that all my life.

"GIVE, AND IT WILL BE GIVEN TO YOU"

But even though I didn't ask people for help, it doesn't mean I did not receive it. I had faithfully given in those prior years, and now, it was coming back to me in awesome, incredible, mysterious ways. There were three distinct events related to: *"A good measure, pressed down, shaken together, running over, will be put into your lap; for the measure you give will be the measure you get back."*

ALL THE BILLS GOT PAID

I didn't publicize my situation, but I didn't hide it, either, and almost immediately, people assisted me. It wasn't easy to receive donations, but I suppressed my pride, accepted the help, and said "thank you" each time. I can't remember everyone and how they assisted, but I was grateful to each and every one of them. I was financially strapped, but all the bills got paid due to unemployment compensation, my wife's new part-time job, and the help from my friends. For instance, my friend Larry, who died of cancer a year later, paid my electric bill for two months. Other friends and family provided funds, gifts, food, etc. I felt like I was being personally cared for and taken care of.

However, things took a peculiar turn in early February: So much money was being donated to me by different people that I had excess funds after paying the bills. This was difficult for me to process. I felt guilty receiving money that I did not genuinely need. My solution was to give away the excess funds to two needy people, including a person with cancer whose financial needs were reported in the newspaper. I don't remember who the second person was. I mailed out the checks, but within three days, I had received back more money from others than I had just given away.

This was one of those literal God-fearing moments where you put your hands up in front of you and take a step back in awe. I gave away no more excess money, and when I returned to work several weeks later, my bank account contained more funds than before the job loss. Let that sink in: I was unemployed for four and a half months and ended up with more money than I started with.

A Christmas Surprise for My Girls

I instructed my wife to spend as much on Christmas gifts for our two young daughters as she typically would. You have seen how important Christmas gifts are to me, so I did not want my girls to suffer because I did not have a job. My wife and I didn't exchange gifts that year, and she bought the girls everything we normally would have.

But then, two days after she had completed the shopping, an anonymous letter arrived in the mail with $100 worth of gift certificates at Toys-R-Us, with a note instructing me to buy gifts for my daughters. The "Geoffrey Dollars" had an expiration date of December 24, so off to the store I went.

And it was difficult spending $50 (in 1992 dollars) on each girl after we had already bought all their planned gifts. It took me ten minutes pushing that full cart around the store one more time to spend the final $5 on that last gift.

RUNNING OVER, INTO YOUR LAP

Both receiving more money than your expenses and buying $100 more Christmas gifts than planned could be considered an overflow of blessings about which THE MAN had decreed. But it is the third event that provides the stunning, complete, literal answer.

THE THREE TURKEYS

When you have always worked and want to work, the stress of unemployment constantly grinds on you. It's difficult to escape it, and it can dominate your life. Although the bills were getting paid, I had much anxiety about my future. I had a family to care for and a daughter with potentially severe medical conditions.

This heavy stress plays tricks on your mind. You begin to think irrationally and become unnecessarily fearful. Looking back on this time, years later, some of these fears are ridiculous, but at the time, they seemed totally reasonable.

As I entered my second month of unemployment in December 1992, the stress really intensified. Job openings are not plentiful before the holidays, so you can't job search as much. But having more free time allows your mind to generate all sorts of false fears.

There were two distressing thoughts constantly rolling around in my head. The first was the fear that I would eventually lose my house, and my family would have to wander homeless in the street.

The second was that I was a failure because I would not be able to provide a turkey for our family Christmas dinner. This idea was preposterous: We had plenty of money to afford a turkey. But that was irrelevant. I saw myself as the family provider, and if I didn't have a job, I would fail to provide this essential part of Christmas.

Now, you may consider this chauvinistic "toxic masculinity", and that's okay. That's how I was raised, and I am not ashamed to admit it. However, it was more toxic than usual in this instance because it ground on me every day as the holiday approached.

"You can't provide a turkey. There may not be a turkey. You have no turkey, none! Your holiday dinner is ruined because there may not be a turkey. It is your responsibility to provide a turkey, and you have failed. You have failed your family. What type of man cannot provide a turkey?"

This hellish "turkey loop" played over and over in my head several times a day, every day. I believe that obsessing over something unimportant is your brain's defense mechanism against obsessing over things that are actually very important. But I was obsessed with a turkey. A turkey for Christmas dinner. Of course, I didn't tell anyone about this fear because I knew it was irrational, yet there it was every day, eating away at me.

A Turkey from Heaven

Two Sundays before Christmas, our Adult Bible Fellowship at church presented my wife and me with five large boxes of food at the end of class. I was up in front thanking people for their generosity when someone came through the door and set a large frozen turkey on the boxes.

Never in my adult life has a small gift made me feel so jubilant. Just as worrying about not having a turkey created enormous sadness, receiving an unexpected turkey produced tremendous joy.

I had a turkey! They gave me a turkey! And I no longer had to worry about it again! I was ecstatic. This is one of my best memories of this time.

It did cause some storage issues, however. We had to store it in our small 90's-sized freezer because it was too soon to thaw it. My wife had to move some stuff around, but she made it fit.

And I was much happier the next week, not worrying about the turkey and instead being joyous over this gift.

Then Friday afternoon, Carl, a guy from church, came to my house. He was out delivering turkeys for the church to needy families. Now, of course, he knew I wasn't "needy", but he had an "extra" turkey and wanted me to have it.

Of course, this was a white lie. If I wasn't considered needy, then what was my name doing on his list? This was just his way of making sure you accepted the turkey. But before I could explain that the church had already provided a turkey, he literally shoved the bird in my chest. I instinctively grabbed it, partially in self-defense. But once I was holding the bird, Carl quickly sprinted back to his car as he shouted, "Merry Christmas!"

I put the second turkey in the fridge and explained how it got there after my wife returned from work. Because Christmas is just a week away, the plan is to start thawing the first turkey in the refrigerator and storing the second turkey in the freezer. We will cook the second turkey in late January and then get our freezer space back.

Two days later, after an afternoon nap, my wife informs me that our friend Dave had stopped by. He had been delivering turkeys for the local food bank to needy families. Of course, we weren't "needy", but guess what? He just happened to have an "extra" turkey, and he wanted us to have it.

If I had been awake, I'm sure I would have tried to reject this third bird. I know I was to accept all gifts, but this was ridiculous. Now, I had too many turkeys. I was overflowing with turkeys, which brings us back to this:

"Give, and it will be given to you. A good measure, pressed down, shaken together, running over, will be put into your

lap; for the measure you give will be the measure you get back."

In eight days, I had received more turkeys than I had capacity for. And you can't press down and shake together frozen turkeys, can you? Turkeys had run over my refrigerator space into my lap.

The question I posed at the beginning of this chapter was: *"How is this statement possible? How could you possibly receive so much you cannot contain it?"* Yet, there I was. The turkeys were overflowing. The strange thing is I don't think I ever explicitly prayed for a turkey. I just worried constantly about it. And then, frozen turkeys began dropping into my lap and overflowing.

But this heavenly provision did cause an earthly problem: I had more turkeys than I could store. So that night, I called my friend Jim, who had a large freezer. After hearing my plight, he graciously agreed to stow two of the turkeys for me. My family enjoyed the second turkey in April and invited Jim and his wife Frannie over for a cookout in August, where we feasted on the final bird.

"Give, and it will be given to you. A good measure, pressed down, shaken together, running over, will be put into your lap; for the measure you give will be the measure you get back."

There are teachings from THE MAN that I still struggle to understand. There are many that I accept by faith. But this one, I don't need to accept by faith, because faith is only in the unseen. This one, I know, is true. I have held the cold evidence in my own hands.

GIVING IN ABUNDANCE FROM ABUNDANCE

"Give, and it will be given to you. A good measure, pressed down, shaken together, running over, will be put into your lap; for the measure you give will be the measure you get back."

I got a new job after being unemployed for nearly five months. It was a relief to have health insurance again for my daughter and resume a stable lifestyle. But I never forgot the three Christmas turkeys or how THE CREATOR's mysterious ways met all my financial needs and more that February. The amazing thing is my bank account was higher at the end of my unemployment than at the beginning. My pastor asked me how that was possible; I really had no explanation.

The lessons of this tribulation stayed with me. It was another life-changing event. The Christmastime giving continued, and I began donating to a ministry that provided holiday gifts to children of needy families. As my children grew older, I donated more money to that ministry than I was spending on them.

And that is fitting because this whole thing started with an image of a child with no presents under the Christmas tree.

At that time, I asked: But what can I do about that?

And my answer now is: I can do this! I CAN DO THIS. I WILL DO THIS.

WHAT YOU LEARN

You learn much by going through the challenging periods of life. You learn you are tough enough to survive them. You learn how to think and utilize resources to overcome obstacles. You learn to grow in your faith. You ultimately learn what you are made of. And the best thing is that what you are made of at the end of your ordeal is much stronger than when it began. Some basketball teams are described as "tournament tough". People who have survived the tough times are "life tough".

And this toughness is so valuable. The next time you're faced with a similar challenge, you won't panic. You won't worry as much. You will know how to handle it. You will have the confidence to overcome it because you have been there and done it before.

If that subsequent trial is even worse, you still will be much better prepared than if you hadn't just survived the last one. Unfortunately, being "life tough" doesn't completely insulate you from a tough life.

THE "THREE TURKEY" TRADITION

Sometime after receiving those three turkeys in 1992, I began giving three turkeys to people in need each December. I didn't provide the actual birds; I would get $20 grocery gift cards early in the month and give them out when I saw a need, sometimes sent anonymously.

But then, something magnificent would happen after I gave away the last card: Within a week or so, I would receive some unexpected money, which coincidently, would be somewhat higher than the $60 I had spent.

One year, I received a check from the IRS for an overpayment. Another year, the college where I was teaching part-time forgot to compensate me for training I had received in May. I wish I had written down the other surprise December payments that came my way, but I never anticipated I would be writing about this 20 years later.

And then, there was the bizarre poker game in December 2008. I had only given away two gift certificates that year and carried around a $20 bill to give to the next needy person who crossed my path. I donated that $20 to a family whose house had just burned down. But that same night, I won $180 in a poker match (More about this in the next chapter).

No turkeys were given away in 2009. The Great Recession had cost me my job again. My circumstances were much less dire since my wife was working now. I did not respond to the situation well, as will be discussed in Chapter 7. But incredibly, for the second time, I came out of unemployment with more money than I started with. And I still can't explain it.

TIME TO RAISE THE BAR

I found a new job, and my finances improved soon afterward. So why limit it to just three turkeys? So, at Christmastime, I started giving ten turkeys away. Then 20, then 30, and last holiday season, with the help of my friend Reverend John, over 70 turkeys. I don't say this to brag—it's just a fact for reference and confirmation of my commitment.

But Don, where did the money come from to donate all those turkeys?

Well, if you don't know the answer, you probably need to reread this chapter!

Because it started with a fundamental truth, which is— one more time, taken slowly:

"Give: freely, generously, with a pure heart when you see people in need of help.

and it will be given to you: you will receive back what you have freely given in some form of blessing or benefit.

A good measure, pressed down, shaken together, running over, will be put into your lap: if your heart and motives have been pure, you will receive back the value of your gift and more. So much more that it overflows.

for the measure you give will be the measure you get back: the intent, the compassion, the generosity, the sacrifice of your giving, will determine the quantity of blessings you receive back.

Oh, and one more thing: Of course, I surely didn't expect to receive back the larger cost to provide 70 turkeys like I did when I gave away just three. Heck, I never expected payback from the three turkeys to begin with—it just happened. But two weeks after giving away the 70 turkeys, my company decided to drop its tremendously expensive health insurance. This allowed me to be covered on my wife's plan. The resulting savings was five times the amount of the check. As I complete my final edit for this book, I wrote my turkey check for 2022.

By the end of the month, I received nine times the value back (in future payments). And I'm retired!

CHAPTER 2:
DEEP, HEAVY CHRISTMAS

Christmas is a big deal to me in so many ways. My fraternal grandmother loved Christmas. I was her only grandchild, so during the nine Christmases we spent together, the magic of the season was passed on to me.

But every Christmas season, I contemplate what Christmas is, what Christmas means, and what difference Christmas should make. As far as the Holidays go, Christmas is deep, heavy stuff.

These writings explore how we need to help others during the Christmas season, as well as all year round. There are essays reflecting on what Christmas was like during the COVID-19 pandemic. These can be compared to old writings during wartime or the Great Depression. Of course, this pandemic was not as bad as those conditions, but it did shake our culture and worldview almost as much. It also affected me and the tone of the essays. The final piece explains why I prefer to say "Merry Christmas" instead of "Happy Holidays", and it provides context for how special the time of year is for me.

KINDNESS WITH A PURPOSE

The Christmas season is approaching, which is excellent for charities. People tend to give more at the end of the year for two reasons: The first is that Christmas reminds us to focus on other people, including the less fortunate, as well as those groups and ministries providing help and aid all around the world. The second is that many donations are tax-deductible, and the tax year is ending. For many givers, the motivation is a combination of both of these.

We know we should help people year-round, but we don't. It's difficult to focus on others in our busy, stress-filled lives. One way people tend to help others throughout the year is to perform "random acts of kindness", such as paying for the person behind them in the drive-thru or for a stranger's check at the diner. You have no doubt seen or heard of these, or you have even been the giver or receiver of one yourself.

These "acts" make the giver feel good. They have done something to help brighten a complete stranger's day, like it's their birthday even when it isn't. And that person might be motivated to pass the gift along, paying for the coffee/food/etc. of the person in line behind them, which creates this massive joy train which makes your latte taste even better.

But ......

I don't like "random acts of kindness".

"Don, are you insane?! 'Random acts of kindness' are terrific! They make me feel so good! What possible problem could you have with this?"

Now, the "kindness" part is excellent. Being kind and doing good deeds are great. It's the whole "randomness" thing I object to. Selecting someone at random who may not even need or want any help doesn't make much sense to me.

Most of the time, the receivers are chosen totally by chance with no consideration of the need. I would feel stupid paying for the coffee of the high-styled woman waiting behind me in her Mercedes. I would get much more enjoyment and satisfaction buying an extra latte for myself.

"Random acts of kindness" are fun, but the thrill comes from the surprise element. It's like a surprise birthday present that is unexpected because it's (most likely) not the person's birthday. The giver feels good, the receiver feels good, but the whole act lacks purpose. In effect, it's really more like unneeded *charity* than kindness.

So if these were called "random acts of charity", it really loses its zing, doesn't it? Few people would write a check and send it to a random, unnamed organization, would they? And is it truly beneficial to be randomly kind to people just because it's fun? Just because we can "humble brag" about it on Facebook? Call me crazy, but I just can't do kindness or charity that way.

I much more prefer "*purposeful* acts of kindness". This concept can be summarized in six words:

See the need— Meet the need

See the need—Meet the need

SEE THE NEED—MEET THE NEED

Understanding and accepting the concept is simple, but actually carrying it out is difficult. In "random acts of kindness", you attempt to meet a need that probably doesn't even exist. In *purposeful* acts of kindness, the challenge is being able to see the person's *actual* needs. This can be very tough to accomplish. In most cases, you can help someone but only after realizing a need exists.

Seeing the needs does not come naturally to us. It is a learned behavior. It requires us to approach life with our eyes wide open. These needs are all around us every day, but we don't see them because we don't look for them. Many of the needs are financial, but some aren't. Some "needs" may be someone to talk to or a shoulder to cry on. Regardless, you must seek to help people whenever you encounter someone in need.

The best example is THE MAN, whose time on Earth could be broadly characterized as traveling around, seeing people's needs, and meeting people's needs. He could even see the needs people didn't even realize they had, and then He still helped them. Of course, He had a supernatural perception to see the needs and an unlimited ability to meet them. But blind people, lame people, sick people, diseased people, distressed people, He helped them all.

Yes, the challenge ...

See the need—Meet the need

See the need—Meet the need

See the need—Meet the need

To see the needs, you must change your mindset. You must train your eyes to look for the needs. It's one of those painfully frustrating things in life where I clearly know what I need to do, but I often fail to do it. I see the needs better when I have time to process the situation. Sometimes I realize too late that there was a need I should have met.

Here are two contrasting examples:

Several years ago, on Father's Day, I had breakfast at a Denny's near Downtown Columbus, Ohio. A man arrived with his two young sons. The oldest is around five years of age.

The mother isn't present. Now, this could be just a "guys-only event" but sending a man out by himself with two young sons can be an adventure. Maybe he's a single father. Perhaps this is a weekend visitation thing. Regardless, in a culture where men routinely abandon their young children and shirk their responsibilities, this guy had chosen to take his two young sons out for breakfast on Father's Day.

See the need – That guy should be rewarded for his effort.

As I passed their booth on the way out, I stopped, smiled, looked at everyone, and placed a $20 bill on the table.

I said, "Happy Father's Day! Breakfast is on me," and left.

Meet the need.

Oh, yes, that looks so impressive, Don!

But let's move on to example two:

In 2020 (but before social distancing), I was standing in line at the service counter at a grocery store, waiting to mail a package. The elderly lady in front of me was having a dispute with the clerk over a charge.

I could only make out bits of the discussion, but it was the type of dispute we all have been involved in: We think we have been unfairly charged and are owed money back, but the store policy dictates we are not getting a refund. The amount in question was around $12. The older woman, of course, kept stating her case and becoming more agitated. The young clerk continued to repeat company policy, growing exasperated. I was becoming impatient, having to wait until this debate ended, knowing my task would only take a short time to complete. Finally, the woman left, upset because she didn't get a refund.

As I walked back to my car, I realized I had failed to see the need and had subsequently failed to meet the need.

As soon as I became aware of the disputed amount, I could have intervened, handed the older woman $12 (or even $20 if I didn't have the exact amount), and wished her a nice day.

Instead of being agitated for the rest of the day and getting upset again telling her friends how horribly that young, uncaring clerk had treated her, she would have been joyous that she'd gotten her $12 back. And the clerk would also be happy that she did not upset an elderly customer by enforcing a store policy, which may not have even been fair to begin with. All the good that could have happened for a mere $12.

In this case, I had failed to see the need, even as it played out right before my eyes. And because I had failed to see the need, I didn't meet the need.

See the need—Meet the need

See the need—Meet the need

See the need—Meet the need

PURPOSEFUL ACT OF KINDNESS – TRY IT NEXT CHRISTMAS

The idea is to replace "random acts of kindness" with "*purposeful* acts of kindness". To do this, we must look for real needs and be ready and prepared to meet those needs quickly, in real time.

It's difficult to "see the needs" in our fast-paced lifestyle when we are often in a hurry. Our culture also prioritizes having our own needs met versus meeting the needs of others. Therefore, we need to plan ahead and have a strategy.

Here is the plan I have used to help me "See the Need" during the Christmas season:

1. Take a $20 bill and designate it as your "Meet the Need" money. At that point, it belongs to someone else. You just don't know who yet.

2. Place the bill somewhere in your change purse or wallet, apart from your other currency. Put it somewhere prominent, where you will see it every time you access your cash or credit cards. Tag it with a paper clip or sticky note if needed.

3. Give the money to the first person you see in need–not a random person in line behind you, but someone who genuinely needs that small

boost. A Purposeful Act of Kindness. You have prepared to see the need and meet the need, so there is no need to think much about the situation—just act.

See the Need—Meet the Need

Prepare your "Meet the Need" money the day after Thanksgiving. You may choose to "reload" if you meet a need early in December.

If you wish, you may ask THE CREATOR to place people with needs in your path because now you are prepared to meet them.

Please put the $20 in your wallet and be ready to See the Need. If you still have the money on Christmas Eve due to limited mobility/social distancing, donate it to the Salvation Army or local food bank.

WHERE THE $20 TRADITION ORIGINATED

Several years ago, I was teaching a marketing course at Indiana Wesleyan University. It was early December and I shared with the class my Story of the Three Turkeys. I explained why I give away turkeys to people in need every Christmas, and also that I had already given away two turkeys that year. The students loved the story up to that point, but then their mood changed.

"Don, you said you received three turkeys in the story, but you only gave away two this year. You owe someone a turkey!"

They were insistent, so I promised them I would give away a third turkey – in the form of a gift card.

But I knew this would be difficult to do. I had given two $20 grocery store gift cards to unemployed friends, but I didn't know anyone else who needed a turkey. It was already mid-December, and I didn't want to face the holiday shoppers to get another gift card. So I took a $20 bill, stuck it in the outside pocket of my money clip, and vowed to give it to the first person I encountered who needed help.

But no prospects crossed my path the following week, and time was running out. My last day in the office before Christmas break was Thursday, and after that, I would have little contact with the general population.

However, Tuesday morning, my coworker Denette sent out a company email asking people in the office to donate money for a local family with five kids whose house and Christmas presents had been destroyed by a fire just days earlier.

And that was it! That was the need I was looking for! However, I had work that was due, so I didn't get over to Denette's desk until late in the day. She got out her collection envelope, and I handed her the $20. She looked down at the eight dollar bills that had been donated, a meager sum considering the office had over 200 workers, as well as how prominent the family's plight had been in the news.

"I don't have enough change for you," she lamented without raising her head.

"No, keep it all," I said.

Her head snaps up, and with a look of deep gratitude, asks, "Really?"

I nod, she thanks me, and I leave.

And that's when the Christmas happens, people.

AND NOW, FOR THE REST OF THE STORY

But there's more to this story. You may enjoy it—or you may not. But I must tell it, regardless.

That night, a few hours after donating that $20, I was at a holiday poker game with a dozen guys from work. It was a friendly, fun time with a modest $20 buy-in. I hadn't played much poker, but this was a most bizarre game.

My luck was atrocious early in the match. I should have been the first player eliminated after only a half hour of play, but somehow through tremendous luck, I was able to survive.

My fortunes then improved a little, but an hour later, I should have been eliminated a second time. However, I got extremely lucky once again and survived. I was then able to scratch and claw back into contention. And then I won the biggest single pot of the night that eliminated two players and left me heads-up against a player whose massive stack of chips dwarfed mine.

He should have squashed me like a bug, but he was inexperienced and made mistake after mistake. He had several opportunities to win the match, but my chips increased. He gave me ample opportunities to catch up to him, and finally, when I won the match, they handed me $200.

It was Wednesday morning when it finally hit me about what had happened at that poker game. I calculated the odds of me winning that match after staving off elimination twice and defeating a much better-funded opponent in heads-up: about one in four million. But in eight hours, I gave $20 to Denette for charity, and someone handed me back $200.

I'm still not entirely sure just what happened that day. It could have been a coincidence, and yet...

I need to put some "Meet the Need" money in my wallet all year long since people do have needs all year long. However, I don't recommend giving this money to "professional panhandlers" who are often seen at highway exits. However, you can make your own decision here.

The important thing here is to be ready. If you are ready to meet the need, it is much easier to meet the need. And never underestimate the value and impact of that action. The person you help may be having a horrible day. They may be mired in the worst situation of their lives. To see that someone cares about their welfare, anyone, can be a huge deal. Be ready to help, and then act.

WE NEED A LOT OF CHRISTMAS NOW
(From Christmas 2020)

The plague of our age has resulted in fear and isolation. We feel held captive and subject to psychological torture. The captors, or those in power, take advantage of these fears to manipulate and indoctrinate the prisoners.

And the people in power, including the leaders of whatever groups are currently screaming the loudest, have used this year to divide us. To divide us by politics, divide us by race, divide us by philosophies, and divide us by religion. Even to divide us by whether we wear face masks. Their goal is to separate us in any way they can.

The powerbrokers do this to acquire more power. If they can manipulate you, then they can control you. They can make you speak and act just like their ventriloquist dummy. Under the stress of the pandemic, everyone is vulnerable to this deception. Because of the plague, they have been able to do this to us all. If you are part of the culture, you have been exposed to it. In some way, even if you aren't aware of it, you have been manipulated.

The result is everyone getting upset at everyone about everything. Everyone is screaming at everyone. This conflict intensifies until we are engulfed in a cesspool of hate. The vitriol generated this year is an abomination. It is a pox upon our souls.

It has now become acceptable in our culture to hate people for very little reason. To hate those you have never met. This culture praises people for their clever hateful statements. There are people whose entire identity in life is to blast people on Twitter. They justify it by thinking hate is good if it is done for a noble reason.

Of course, they tell themselves, *"My reasons are always just, pure, and moral, just as I am. And anyway, they started it."*

But every derisive statement we make, every snarky comment, every proud post, and every nasty tweet only generates more hate.

This year, the deadliest pathogen is not the transmission of a virus, from which most recover, but the spread of hate, from which we may never recover.

There is a vaccine for the virus, and the pandemic will eventually cease. But the hate? It will rage on. In the words of Bob Dylan, what we need is "a shot of love".

The virus separated us from our fellow humans, and then our gods and captors took advantage of the turmoil and divided us. Socially distanced, we are now staying six feet away. But relationally distanced, we are 600 miles apart.

And into this sewer of hate, during the fury of the $h!tstorms, enters Christmas. You may believe the holiday is ruined this year, but Christmas exists for a reason—just not the reason you think.

The Christmas message is simple by design. When we complicate it in any way, we dilute its power. This message is not just for the faithful but for *every* person, *everywhere.* You don't have to believe the story to accept the principle woven throughout.

And that principle is so basic yet so powerful: We are to love our brothers and sisters—*all* people—not hate them. We need this reminder so desperately this year as the pandemic rages.

Christmas can be explained in just one word: "*Emmanuel*", which is unfolded in our language as "God is with us". If God is with us—with us *all*—then the farther we move away from each other because of our divisions and prejudices, the farther we all move away from God.

So you see, the princes in power aren't just separating us from each other. At the same time, they are separating us from God. This has tremendous damaging effects. We are being fed a steady diet of poison, and it is killing us. It is destroying our souls.

What would happen today if God was literally with us—again? Would we receive the gentle rebuke? Or would the voting machines get thrown down, as the tables were outside the temple? Would the news stations crumble? Would the protest signs be thrown in the fire? Which practices and institutions would receive the most reproach?

Christmas has arrived at the perfect time this year. If ever we needed God to be with us, it is right now.

We need to stop the hate.

We need to stop the hate.

We need to stop the hate.

O come all ye faithful, as well as ye who are not faithful at all, and put a stop to this.

Please stop this now.

The uniting message of Christmas is that if God is with us and we are with God, we are closely bonded with each other. It doesn't get any plainer or more direct than that.

It is time to put away all the garbage you have collected this year. To wash off the filth and mud from the derisive arguments. It's Christmastime, and it's time to come together. It's time to extend those tidings of comfort and joy to your enemies as well as your friends.

And for that, we can truly rejoice.

IS YOUR CHRISTMAS RUINED THIS YEAR? (2021)

You've heard the news reports lamenting that Christmas will be ruined due to product shortages caused by backups at the West Coast ports.

But Christmas should not be limited by the amount of stuff you can buy or get.

Christmas joy should not be contained within shipping containers sitting on the docks.

However, our culture emphasizes *stuff*. Everyone is trying to get more *stuff*. Even though most of us have way more stuff than we need, we crave more. And many people use Christmas as a reason to get much more stuff.

Christmas is the most *religious* holiday by far. If you are more traditional in your ways, you worship the birth of THE MAN. If your god happens to be money-stuff, you celebrate by buying, giving, and receiving as much stuff as possible.

We are motivated, manipulated, and cheered on in these festivities by the television commercials that proclaim this to be the season to hoard anything and everything we can. It is intriguing that none of these advertisers actually mention the "reason for the season," carefully using every euphemism in the book to avoid saying...

Christmas.

They can't actually say His name because that would be messy. They don't want to expose their exploitation of something so pure.

Besides, someone could get offended... and they still need that someone to buy their stuff. Lots and lots of *stuff*.

The culture has combined the original Pagan roots of the solstice/Saturlina festival with the commemoration of THE MAN's birth. And being the highly inclusive people that we are, you have the freedom to celebrate as you prefer.

Now, there are plenty of ways to find merriment at Christmastime, and we all celebrate in our personal ways. The three main ways are:

The spiritual aspect, which includes charity that results from faith.

Family and traditions.

The giving and getting of stuff.

To maximize your Christmas joy, you need a balance of all three (forgive me for channeling my economist mind). Overemphasizing any of these lessens the impact. If it's all just the "spiritual" part, you miss out on the fun of the traditions and some of the stuff. This is equivalent to being invited to THE MAN's birthday party but not being allowed to have any fun. You also lose some joy if you get too hooked on just the traditions (People with thousand-dollar light displays and overzealous cookie-bakers, I'm talking to you—perhaps diverting some of the expense and effort to charity could help).

Which brings us back to the "*stuff*". The harmful result of being committed, attracted, and addicted to the *stuff* is that you will value the *stuff* over people. We have seen the videos of people fighting over products on Black Friday (the holy day for stuff lovers). Men and women alike have been punched, shoved, trampled, and otherwise injured in their pursuit of the "hottest" gifts.

Our sad condition, where stuff—including money, the means to buy the stuff—is much more important than people, is our culture's greatest failing and weakness. The message that "greed is good" is pounded into us every day—and unfortunately, more in December than at any other time of the year.

It is so easy to allow your money to become your god. Money provides you with stuff, and the Christmas season seemingly gives you permission to buy all the stuff you want and can. Even more than that if you max your credit cards. You can naturally worship the god of money at this time without even realizing it. Just remember, everyone worships a God, or gods, so be extremely careful what you choose to worship.

Which brings us back to Christmas. If there is one universal message of Christmas—and this is true whether you consider the story itself truth or fable—it is that people are more important than stuff. And similarly, nothing is more important than people.

As we read about THE MAN, we see that He always put the needs of people first. He NEVER, EVER valued stuff more than people.

Not once. Not one time.

This truth should influence our behavior around the holidays and all year round. It should impact our interaction with strangers, our relationships, our charitable acts, and even our political views. It should even cause us to evaluate who should be admired more: the CEO of the large corporation, or the guy who runs the soup kitchen downtown?

If bare shelves and stockouts can ruin your Christmas, maybe you are doing it wrong.

It Will Always Be "Merry Christmas" For Me

Merry Christmas!

or more specifically ...

Merry Christmas to you!

or more completely ...

I wish you a Merry Christmas!

I won't say "Happy Holidays" because in actuality, that would include wishing you a Happy Flag Day. And while I hope your June 14th is pleasant, I prefer to be much more specific about celebrations in December.

And Christmas is set apart from all other holidays. It reaches a much higher realm—even, might I say, an angelic one.

For we say: *Happy Valentine's Day, Happy St. Patrick's Day, Happy Independence Day, Happy Labor Day, Happy Halloween, Happy Thanksgiving, Happy Hanukkah, Happy Kwanzaa,* and *Happy New Year.*

But we wish people a *Merry* Christmas. It is not just *happy*—it is *merry.* There is merriment—joyfulness, cheerfulness, vivaciousness, jolliness, mirth, hilarity, and laughter. Many things in life make you happy; very few things make you truly merry.

So, Merry Christmas!

I wish you a Merry Christmas!

I am not trying to change your beliefs when I say this. There is no ulterior motive. I am choosing to share with you the joy I possess and the merriment I experience at Christmastime. Because it is Christmas, and Christmas means so much to me.

And this expression of joy is universally inclusive because I will offer this greeting to anyone. It goes out to all races, all nations—to Muslims, to Hindus, to atheists. Everybody gets a dose of my Christmas spirit. Even people I don't like (Obnoxious coworkers in my past, I'm talking to you)!

Even if you don't believe as I do, I hope you will still be able to experience the merriment. If you think it is a myth, I will still wish you a Merry Christmas. For this was either the most incredible event in the history of mankind or the greatest tale ever created by man's mind. Either way, it is worthy of a grand celebration.

It is so special, so monumental, so blessed that when I wish you a Merry Christmas...

I wish you **love**—that your broken relationships are healed, and new relationships are kindled. That you have people who care about you and whom you care about. That you love, and receive love back in abundance.

I wish you **joy**—that the people, circumstances, and events in your life make you more than happy. That they provide lasting joy beyond the Christmas season.

I wish you **peace**—yes, that same "peace on Earth, goodwill toward all men" that you have heard about. World peace, so that the nations will not battle and innocent people will not perish. And personal peace, so those worries and fears within your head will cease.

I wish you **kindness**—that people will be kind to you when you make mistakes, react poorly, are rude to them, or are vulnerable. And that you extend kindness to others in the same circumstances.

I wish you **generosity**—in that when you need help, someone will provide that help. And when you see others in need, you will give freely and generously to meet that need.

I wish you a Merry Christmas!

I wish you happiness, and merriment, and all the jolliness of this season. I wish that at least for one day this year, you can forget about all the disease, political toxicity, pain, arguments, and worries of the world, and instead focus on and experience the wonder of Christmas.

Merry Christmas!

I wish you a Merry Christmas!

And if somehow, you choose to reject all of this—if it upsets or offends you—that's not on me...

However, it just might be worth taking another look at the whole thing.

Merry Christmas! Merry Christmas! Merry Christmas!

CHAPTER 3: WELCOME TO FATHERHOOD (FOR NOW)

By itself, becoming a first-time father is a life-changing event. However, throw in some randomly horrible circumstances, and the degree of change becomes exponential. In an imperfect world, imperfect stuff happens, even on what you think is the greatest day of your life. Often, these imperfect events are deep, heavy stuff.

This is the most painful piece I have ever written, even more painful than writing my mother's obituary. I share what it was like to go from one of the best days of my life to the absolute worst—all in just a 28-hour period. I describe the worst of it in brutally honest detail, including everything going on inside my head.

As always, these essays are accurate retellings to the best of my recollection. I do realize that medical technology and procedures have improved over the past thirty-some years, so there may be some technical errors.

I never wanted to write about this, but here it is.

Before I wrote the essay titled "300", I told this part of the story for the first time ever to my friend, the Reverend John.

I asked him, "Can I actually write this?"

"You have to," he replied, "because it is a story of hope, and somebody needs to hear it."

So you can either believe this story, or you can dismiss it to chance. It doesn't matter to me.

It's my story. I now own it.

WELCOME TO FATHERHOOD

On a Saturday morning in October 1985, my first child was born. We named her Allison. I was in the delivery room, but I didn't observe much of the miracle itself because I get very queasy very easily.

I am not, nor have I ever been good in hospitals. This is important information for later.

However, it was a normal birth with no unexpected issues. After spending some time with my wife and new daughter, I headed home, totally immersed in the euphoria of becoming a father for the first time.

The first sign of trouble came that same evening when my wife called to inform me that Allison had been transferred to Akron Children's Hospital. However, this didn't alarm me at all; during our child-birthing classes, they had told us that babies get transferred there all the time for minor, routine ailments and, if that happened to ours, not to worry.

So I wasn't concerned, although I was still upset. It would delay us bringing Allison home and, almost as importantly, interfere with my schedule. This is an example of how selfish I was at the time—I'd been a young man back then, after all—but this, among other things, was about to change drastically.

The next morning, I went to church and received the joyous congratulations of all my friends, still basking in the exhilaration of being a new father.

After lunch, I headed back to the hospital to see my wife.

I did find it odd that my wife was not in her room, but I still wasn't concerned. I sat down and waited, watching the Cleveland Browns game on a 5" hospital television.

However, as the minutes passed, I began to feel uneasy.

Eventually, a nurse appeared. She seemed surprised to see me there.

With a blank expression, she asked, "Mr. Ake?"

I nodded.

"Please follow me."

Before I could ask why, she spun out of the room, and I struggled to catch up with her.

By this time, I sensed something was wrong. The feeling of impending doom had arrived. It would be an extended stay.

She led me to a "family waiting room" where my wife and her parents were sitting. They were distraught. They uttered half-hearted greetings and returned to staring at the floor.

I knew that my daughter wasn't dead because no one was crying, but things had to be bad.

Really, really bad.

When I asked what was wrong, my wife held up her hand and told me to wait for the doctor. She couldn't tell me the answer herself. It was too painful.

The doctor soon appeared and informed me—with a cold, blank expression and a somber voice—that my daughter had suffered a severe cerebral hemorrhage at birth.

He then delivered the following prognosis:

1. Your daughter probably won't survive today.

2. If she survives today, she probably won't survive tomorrow.

3. If she survives tomorrow, there is a critical time in two weeks that she will have to get through.

4. If she makes it through that, she will live with severe brain damage.

In other words...

"Welcome to fatherhood, Don. I hope you enjoy it because it looks like it's not going to last very long."

THE VALLEY OF THE SHADOW OF DEATH

Yea, though I walk through the valley of the shadow of death, I will fear no evil ...

This is just about the worst news any new parent can receive. Even being told your child is dead has some finality and can be the start of a recovering point. But my news was like being emotionally tortured until every last bit of sanity is extracted from your mind. It was like living in Hell on Earth, and there wasn't a darn thing I could do about it.

I was completely devastated. I returned to my chair, trying not to hyperventilate.

No one uttered a word. Everyone was in too much pain.

Few things in life can shake your core as hard as this. It's one of those rare moments when you become engulfed in every negative emotion at once: pain, fear, anger, grief, despair, anguish, heartbreak, anxiety, and panic—lots of panic.

My brain felt like it was on fire, randomly sending surges of emotional pain and turbulence throughout my body, and there was no way to stop it. My emotions raged like a hurricane, spiraling out of control.

And there were no prayers, either silently or as a group. Because in this situation, exactly what do you pray for? To pray, you need hope, even an ounce of it. Asking THE MAN for help implied that this was just a roadblock we needed to overcome. However, there was nothing blocking the edge of a cliff with no way to go but down.

I literally didn't have a prayer. Only pain. Lots of pain.

The situation was hopeless. There was nothing to do but sit in that hospital waiting room, wait for that inevitable phone call with the inevitable bad news, and then cry and wail. That seemed logical, but it was the easy way out.

But even though my status as a father was extremely fragile (and, I feared, brief), in that moment, I was still a father. And despite my internal torment, I begin to think like a father. My fatherly instincts, which I didn't know existed before then, kicked in.

Fathers protect their children. Fathers provide for their children. Fathers fix things for their children. Men are wired to take action in crisis situations. I felt the need to respond, but what could I possibly do?

In all that turmoil, I heard a voice. It said to remember the man's daughter from the Book of Mark (from THE BOOK)*.

The man's name is Jairus. The doctor tells him that his twelve-year-old daughter is going to die. He rushes to find THE MAN and convinces Him to come help his daughter. The story ends with the dead girl being brought back to life.

In this story, we tend to focus on the miracle that happens at the end, and we skim past all that must have happened to make that miracle possible. Jairus was a leader in the local synagogue. His bosses would not have approved of his actions. His friends probably thought he was crazy and told him not to seek out THE MAN. But here, we have a father who loved his daughter so much that he risked his job, status, and reputation on the sliver of hope he could save his daughter. Without those actions, there would have been no story—none. There would have been no miracle, and the girl would have remained dead.

A SLIVER OF HOPE

Now, I had that sliver of hope, and the great thing about hope is that you don't need much to make a difference. I might lose, but I wasn't going down without a fight. Like Jairus, I would do whatever I could.

And this makes a big difference. One moment, I'm content to sit there until my daughter dies. The next, I can't. I knew I had to do something—anything! My adrenaline started pumping, and suddenly, I was able to focus. But I would not and could not just sit in that room any longer.

I sprung up and announced, "I'm going over to Children's Hospital to see Allison."

And it was an announcement. A proclamation. A declaration, even.

My wife and my in-laws are stunned by this statement. Because, let me reiterate, I never functioned well in hospitals, and everyone knew it. Sometimes, I can get nauseous and light-headed even when just visiting friends. Under these dire circumstances, no one expected me to go there now. This action was completely out of character for the Don Ake they knew, but fatherhood changes a man. In this case, within thirty minutes under a high-pressure situation, I was transformed into a completely different man. It was time to step up, even if I didn't expect to be a father much longer.

Once I made this decision, I was in a mad rush to get to my daughter. I bolted out of the hospital and jumped in my car. It was one of the most challenging drives of my life. I was not fully in control of my emotions or senses. It was dangerous to drive in that condition. Fortunately, the trip to the children's hospital is just over half a mile. However, I hit every agonizing red light.

At the final red light, I started hyperventilating and had to lean forward onto the steering wheel. Fortunately, I was able to keep my foot on the brake.

And it was during this short trip that I offered up the first prayer for my daughter. However, it was not a good prayer. In fact, it's the type of prayer we should *never* do. We are never supposed to bargain with THE CREATOR. It is always wrong to do that. However, I was delirious and not focused on saying a righteous, appropriate, holy prayer. I've now got that sliver of hope, and if you have any hope at all, you've got a prayer. So, as flawed and as misguided as it was, I just blurted it out loud:

"God, if you let her live, I promise I will raise her the best that I can."

I get to Children's Hospital, and there are the typical series of delays:

I must show I.D.

Then, I must find the ICU.

I finally get to the waiting area, but I still can't proceed because I have to "prep". I can still remember vigorously scrubbing my hands with the surgical-grade soap; it felt good to burn up some of the nervous energy.

I put on a protective gown over my clothes and then waited some more for the nurse to return.

I anxiously stand there, resisting the temptation to burst through that door and find my daughter.

WELCOME TO THE VALLEY OF THE SHADOW OF DEATH

Finally, the nurse reappears and motions for me to enter. It is a large room with rows of over 100 sick babies, most in isolettes (clear plastic-enclosed cribs).

My anxiety level rises. I started to doubt whether this was a good idea. Every one of these babies has parents, and every one of these parents is going through a Hell on Earth similar to mine. It is the most depressing scene I have ever encountered.

There is a specific order to where the babies are placed in the ICU: The patients are initially assigned spots based on the seriousness of their condition and, as they improve, are moved right to left towards the door. The closer you are to the door, the closer you are to leaving the ICU.

The nurse turns right and leads me down the front aisle at a good pace. Walking through a room of sick babies hits me hard.

I begin to realize the gravity of the moment: This is a place of life and a place of death. And now I can see the shadow. I can feel the shadow. I can smell the shadow. Yea, I am walking into the valley of the shadow of death.

The nurse keeps walking. All the way down to the last row of isolettes on the wall farthest away from the door.

We turn left, and she stops.

I might have thought I was prepping in that waiting area. But I assure you, there is nothing, absolutely nothing in life, that could have ever prepared me for this.

FEARING THE EVIL

I follow the nurse down to the row against the back wall where the most critical babies are located. We turn the corner, and in the middle of the row, I see the name "Allison Ake" on an isolette. The nurse keeps walking, but I stop a good five feet away. Stunned by what I see, I can't take another step.

The nurse spins around and is surprised that I'm still standing in the aisle. She quickly backtracks and asks, "Can I get you anything, Mr. Ake?"

"Yes, I need a glass of water and a chair. Oh, and please bring the chair now."

As I answered her question, my eyes never left the isolette. Most fathers delight in seeing their day-old daughter, but I am staring at the most horrible scene of my entire life.

My daughter is lying in that isolette. Her arms are raised up, firmly against the sides of her head, her fists tightly clenched. Eyes shut, she struggles for every breath, and there are tubes and wires everywhere.

I still haven't moved. I've stopped instinctively because I'm in a dangerous situation, like when you get too close to a blazing fire or a ferocious animal. But in those instances, you would immediately back away or even run. And I want to turn and run, but I can't because the name on the isolette says "Allison Ake" and that means this one, no matter how damaged, belongs to us.

It is much more than a gut-punch. It's as if a warhead has been fired right through me, removing my gut but leaving me alive to deal with the pain. I stand there frozen, but inside, my heart is racing as I try to absorb the stone-cold reality sitting before me.

The nurse returns with the chair and places it beside the isolette because of course, I can't sit in the aisle. I take the four steps forward and slide quickly into the chair as I feel my knees weaken. I sit slumped over, staring at the floor, as the nurse leaves to get my water.

The nurse returns, and I take a gulp.

"Mr. Ake, do you have any questions?" she asked.

Now, you would think the obvious question is, "How is she doing?" But even though I have only been a father for just a little over twenty-four hours, I am in Full Dad Mode.

"What's wrong with her arms? Why are they raised above her head?" I asked.

"The cerebral hemorrhage your daughter suffered causes intense seizures," she explained. "She put up her arms to fight off the shocks to her brain, and they locked in that position. It's rare to survive seizures that intense, but she did. She's a fighter."

I stare at the nurse in disbelief, just as I had when the doctor had given me the prognosis earlier. The nurse returned to her duties. I sipped some more water, and the emotions started raging out of control again. I just wanted to scream, but I couldn't because that would have distracted the doctors and nurses from doing their jobs.

I turned and looked at Allison, my face inches from the isolette—

Breathe in ... Breathe out ... Breathe in ... Breathe out ...

Here, time is measured in breaths, and at the back wall of the ICU, every breath is vital.

I felt some fatherly pride. This tiny, day-old kid had fought off certain death. And it's not surprising that the offspring of two strong-willed, stubborn people had not died when she was supposed to. I vowed to stay there with her all night—if she makes it through the night.

However, I wasn't prepared for all the intensity against the back wall of the ICU. The monitoring alarms for the critical babies randomly sounded every ten minutes or so. Every time, it was an emergency or life-threatening situation, and six doctors and nurses rushed to that isolette to keep that baby alive. As things stabilized, one by one, they leave to tend to the other infants.

It is like sitting in the middle of Hell. Every time this scene is repeated, it sent a shock through me, never knowing if that baby was going to survive and never knowing if Allison's alarm would be the next to sound. It was a psychological torture chamber that I wouldn't wish upon my worst enemy.

Even though I'd told myself I would stay with her all night, under that stressful environment, I lasted just two hours, and I was disappointed with myself. I took a long look at Allison before leaving. I realized it might be my last look ever, but I sensed I would be coming back. I returned to the first hospital to report back and comfort my wife.

I went home that night to an empty house, feeling much different than when I left nine hours earlier. I was alone and horrified.

I lay down in bed, terrified. Six hours later, I open my eyes, and I am still just as terrified.

I called my wife and am relieved to hear that Allison had survived through the night.

I returned to that torture chamber on day two. You must give me credit—that is the worst place I have ever been in my life, yet I willingly returned. I still needed the chair, but not the water.

And she's still breathing ...

Breathe in ... Breathe out ... Breathe in ... Breathe out ...

It's still brutal to sit in the ICU again with those monitor alarms going off. I only last about the same two hours again. But I don't see any other parents visiting the back wall, so I don't feel as guilty this time.

King David writes in THE BOOK: *"Yea, though I walk through the valley of the shadow of death, I will fear no evil."* **

And you don't grasp the magnitude of those words until you have to take that walk yourself. Because every step that I take, I am surrounded, maybe engulfed, by evil. It is ever present and ever threatening, every second of the day. And David is a much stronger man than I, for I do fear the evil. I fear the evil with every breath I take. I am more fearful than I have ever been in my life.

But Allison does make it through day two. The immediate threat has passed—a huge victory, given the dire odds. The next eleven days bring a series of small victories. She lowers her arms to a normal position. She opens her eyes. And her isolette is moved a few rows forward, finally off that perilous back wall.

I started to feel much better about the situation. At last, I can breathe normally again. At last, the stress is easing. I can finally see some light at the end of this dismal tunnel. My hope has risen, and I felt that exhilaration of beating those terrifically long odds, when everyone literally leaves you for dead and yet you still survive. We had narrowly dodged two bullets, and I felt bulletproof.

However, if you remember the prognosis, the doctor warned us about a critical point occurring in two weeks. Of course, I forget all about this danger because I was so focused on her daily progress.

But a third projectile was fired at Allison. And this was a missile, not a bullet. There would be no dodging this one.

"300"

(As I mentioned earlier, I'd kept this part of the story secret for thirty-five years before discussing it with the Reverend John, gathering the courage to post it on Deep Heavy Stuff, and finally, including it in this book.)

The day after Allison was born, the doctor delivered the following prognosis:

1. Your daughter probably won't survive today.

2. If she survives today, she probably won't survive tomorrow.

3. If she survives tomorrow, there is a critical time in two weeks that she   will have to get through.

4. If she makes it through that, she will live with severe brain damage.

We had made it over the first two hurdles fine. Allison was progressing well, considering the circumstances. I started to feel much better and was incredibly hopeful.

But it was a false hope.

The doctor never explained the complications Allison would face at the two-week juncture because she was not expected to still be alive. And I didn't ask about it because I was overwhelmed by the immediate danger. But the doctor didn't say there "may" be a critical time. He said, "there is".

And now that almost two weeks had passed, the doctor explained the danger in very stark terms:

The cerebral hemorrhage Allison suffered causes her brain fluid to thicken. She will need a shunt inserted into her brain (the same type used for hydrocephalus patients) to drain out the contaminated fluid. If the fluid isn't drained, pressure builds up in the brain, leading to a slow, painful death.

However, the doctor needs the thickness of the brain fluid to be at 200 mg/dL (milligrams per deciliter) for this operation to have a good chance of success; they won't even operate if the reading is above 300. If the fluid is above 300 mg/dL, you are caught in a literal deathtrap: An operation is needed to drain the thick fluid out of the brain, but if the fluid is too thick, they can't operate. The body does generate new fluid every day and drains out what old fluid it can. So, they run an initial test to see how thick Allison's fluid is and then repeat the tests every other day to chart her progress.

On Thursday, they run the first test, and our family and friends begin praying that Allison will be able to have the operation that could save her life. My prayer was a little different than that, however. I am analytical by nature, and the Baptists instruct you to pray very specifically. I pray that the test will be at 300. This is prayed without ceasing. It is prayed repeatedly and fervently.

Over and over: 300, 300, 300, 300.

The first fluid is drawn on Thursday, and on Friday, we learned her fluid was at a reading of 720. This is terrible news. A 720 reading is a long way from 300, but it was only one data point. We won't know how fast this fluid is draining until we get a second reading. But I do know it is a race against time. This is extreme, maximum pressure. Life and death, with a timer counting down.

I continued to pray:

300, 300, 300, 300.

They drew more fluid on Saturday. On Sunday, we waited anxiously for the test results. The phone rang just before 7 pm. My wife took the call, then turned to me and said, "The test came in at 690."

Instantly, I realized the literal gravity of the situation. Now I had a second data point, but there is nothing to analyze. You can do the math without a calculator: The fluid thickness had only gone down 30 points in two days. It needed to go down another 390 points. At this rate, it would take 26 more days to reach 300, and I'm not sure she had another 24 hours.

It was over. It was so over. There had always been that flicker of hope, that tiny candle burning in the night. But now, even that light had been extinguished. There was only darkness. Even the shadow in this valley of death was covered by the night. I was once again devastated.

"I'm going for a walk," I blurt out, as I grab my coat and bolt out the door.

I was walking as fast as I ever have, yet I was not going particularly anywhere. I'm not in control of my movements. I was beyond angry—this was all-out rage. The anger had been building up within me for two weeks. I hadn't dealt with it because there was too much going on. This enormous fury had just built up inside me and now it was being unleashed all at once. I was so enraged I couldn't think straight. It hurt so darn much that I cried for the first time in this trial. I was glad it was dark so anyone out that night couldn't see my horribly distressed face.

I turned back for home after about a mile because if I didn't, I might just keep walking away. At that point, I have burned off most of the raw emotion and begin to think clearly again. But I was still enraged at everyone and everything, and especially at THE CREATOR. We had made it through the long odds, and now after going through two weeks of hell, this was going to end with her slow, painful death. That is unacceptable to me. So, if prayer is loosely defined as "communicating with God," then I guess I said a prayer.

Exactly what I prayed will remain between me and THE CREATOR. I would rate it as my worst prayer ever, but it was also my most honest. I unloaded all that rage— every bit, just dumped it all out.

I am about three minutes from home when I finish this awful prayer. And then something weird occurs: My soul gets quiet. I was at peace. For the first time since this hellish trip began, I regained control of my emotions.

I was willing to accept the inevitable no matter how painful it would be. There would be no more prayers for "300".

That evening, I started thinking about life beyond the inevitable:

What will the funeral be like?

How long will it take my wife and I to recover from this?

Can our marriage even survive this tragedy?

I went to work Monday morning knowing there was a good chance my phone would ring sometime that week, and the struggle would be over. Of course, this is before the days of cellphones, so every time my office phone rings, I held my breath before answering and then exhaled when it turned out to be a business call.

It was a variation of Russian Roulette played with a phone instead of a gun.

But I didn't have to wait long. Around 9:45 on Tuesday morning, my wife called. Instinctively, I grabbed the edge of my desk with my right hand, bowed my head, and closed my eyes, bracing for the worst.

However, my wife called to tell me the results of the Monday fluid test. I had forgotten they had even drawn more fluid. Why even bother? We were 390 points away from 300. It seemed pointless. More bad news would just add to the torture as we counted down to the end.

However, my wife was excited and talking so fast that I couldn't understand what she said.

I asked her to slow down and repeat it.

This time I clearly hear her words, but I can't comprehend what I heard.

I asked her to repeat it one more time.

"The test came in at 300," she said, slightly irritated at having to deliver the message a third time. "She's scheduled for emergency surgery tomorrow morning."

After the call ends, I sat there with my head still bowed, holding the receiver in my hand, trying to process the inconceivable news I have just received. I am stunned, and I begin to shake.

It took a few minutes to regain my composure, and I informed my boss that I would be out of the office on Wednesday. While this is great news, it just meant my two-week-old daughter could undergo delicate brain surgery, which still had a limited chance of success since she just made the minimum requirement for the procedure.

LOOKING FOR A "HOW"

Yes, something miraculous happened, but I am no one special. I am not uniquely or specially blessed here. If I were, I wouldn't have been in this situation to begin with, nor do I possess any type of superior faith. This is evident when my wife tells me the reading is 300.

My first reaction—my very first reaction—is to ask, "Did the doctor say how that happened?"

The question perturbs my wife. "No, they didn't say anything," she snaps back.

Because she doesn't care *how* it happened—it's just wonderful news. Even the doctor doesn't care *how* it happened, he just knows he has been given the opportunity to save a life that he thought was lost. I'm the only person searching for a "how".

But my wife had not been praying specifically for 300, and the doctor had not been expecting 300. I had been the one praying for 300, and I had been the one who knew that achieving 300 was not possible because it was impossible for the reading to drop from 690 to 300 in two days. Oh, I needed to know *how* this happened.

I must conclude that the laws of physical nature have been superseded, and I guess that might be a different way of defining a miracle. Given the information, I do not believe the thick fluid started draining out of her brain at an increased rate. This means the fluid did not gradually dilute from 690 mg/dL to 300 over two days; it had to have changed in an instant. And there are examples in THE BOOK detailing the instant transformation of fluids, including water into wine, and the cleansing of a woman with an "issue of blood" which, interestingly, occurs in the Jarius narrative mentioned earlier.

Now, if you doubt my conclusion, you are forced to come up with various physical explanations of how the test could have dropped to 300 from 690 in two days. And that's fine, go right ahead. I will not argue with you. However, do realize that it takes as much faith to believe in whatever explanation you devise as it does to believe that THE CREATOR interceded. And just be careful about what you choose to put your faith in.

I had prayed specifically for 300, and now I am dealing with a result of 300. Consider that it is not 290. It is not 310. It is *exactly* 300. It is as precise an answer to a prayer as you're ever going to get. And again, it is not the result of any great amount of faith. It is literally amazing grace.

Now, you might think someone who received such a direct answer to prayer would run up and down the street proclaiming the news. Maybe shout it from the rooftops. But I respond to encountering the presence of

THE CREATOR more like Isaiah, who proclaims in THE BOOK, "*Woe is me. I am doomed.*"***

Regardless, I had no time to proclaim anything because there was emergency surgery scheduled for tomorrow.

Early Wednesday morning, my wife and I met with the doctor to discuss the operation. It is delicate. It is risky. Eighteen days ago, I could not even comprehend being able to keep my composure in that hospital waiting room while doctors perform brain surgery on my infant daughter. But there I was. I am growing up into an adult by necessity.

Oh, yes, I was nervous. Yes, I was anxious. And yes, it was physically and mentally draining. But there was one emotion missing now that had been present that entire time.

"Yea, though I walk through the valley of the shadow of death, I will fear no evil."

The shadow of death was still there. The evil was still there. But the fear is gone.

You see, the keyword in that passage is not "death", nor "fear", nor "evil". The only word that means anything here is *through*. The statement of faith David is making is that he is going to make it *through* this.

This is going to be a brutal walk. There is going to be incredible pain. Evil is present everywhere. But he is walking *through* it. No matter what happens in that valley, he is confident that he will emerge on the other side.

And this is a process. When you enter this dark valley, you are more afraid than you have ever been in your entire life. But at some point, in this perilous walk, you are forced to stare the evil in the face. And then you have a choice: You can either cower in fear or choose to walk on by faith. Faith may really be the opposite of fear. You leave behind the valley of the shadow of death a much different person than when you entered.

I matured as a man more in those eighteen days than in any other time in my life. It is literally a defining moment. It changed my view of life, how I respond to crises, how I interact with people. Those eighteen days changed me forever.

The operation was a complete success, without any near-term complications. I was confident it would be; since Allison had beaten the long odds so many times, I had come to expect it.

And yet, the prize for making it over the first three hurdles is this:

#4. If she makes it through all that, she will live with extensive brain damage.

There is no escaping the fact that Allison had significant brain damage, which typically results in severe cerebral palsy.

However, the story didn't end there...

THE EPILOGUE

After her surgery, Allison returned to the ICU and stayed there for two more weeks to recover. But she was now much closer to the door, much closer to coming home.

During this time, we had a meeting with the neurologist to review her condition. The doctor knew it was going to be a difficult discussion for all of us, so he decided to give us the good news up front.

"We think she can see!" he said with enthusiasm.

"What?" I blurted out.

This was my typical reaction since day one of this ordeal. Someone unexpectedly gives me horrible news that I can't believe. In this case, the doctor thought I was doubting him.

"No, we think she can see. The nurses say her eyes are following their movements," he explained.

He then whips out her brain scan and proceeded to point out all the problems. I glanced down at the image, but then raised my eyes and studied only his expressions. I may not be able to read a brain scan, but I can read the face of someone who must deliver horrible news to a young couple about their infant daughter.

It was all bad news. The brain damage was extensive. I learned more about the functions of the human brain that day than I ever wanted to. The vision success was the only bright spot, and the doctor was truly surprised by that because of the damage to Allison's optic nerve.

We brought Allison home a couple of days before Thanksgiving. It was the best Thanksgiving ever because there was so much to be thankful for.

And so, the task of raising Allison began.

However, if you remember, there was a promise made the day after she was born, when I was driving that strenuous half-mile to the Children's Hospital to see her:

"God, if you let her live, I promise I will raise her the best that I can."

I reiterate: You should never make conditional promises to THE CREATOR. You should never bargain with THE CREATOR.

Never. Period.

However, if you find yourself in a dire situation and, out of desperation, you spontaneously make a conditional promise to THE CREATOR, and if by some bizarre, even miraculous means, THE CREATOR fulfills his part of your bargain, then you had better keep your promise.

Period.

So I began to fulfill my part of the bargain. The doctors had us focus on Allison's mental development, probably because they believed her physical capabilities were limited. They instructed us to read to her regularly, even though she could not comprehend yet. Therefore, I would place her near me and read my newspaper or magazine out loud to her. One time, my wife yelled at me when I was reading to her from an article in *Psychology Today* dealing with adult issues.

But then, another chapter in this incredible story started to unfold: Allison began to progress much better than the doctors expected. Allison was developing mentally at what seemed like a normal pace, and while there were physical issues, she exhibited decent mobility.

I questioned her primary care physician about this. He explained that when a child suffers brain damage at birth, sometimes their body is able to rewire itself and assign some functions to the healthy brain cells, cells that typically would not be used for anything. The result: Although Allison has severe brain damage as the neurologist had shown us, she has only moderate cerebral palsy.

Raising a child with special needs is challenging. There were numerous operations (including three additional brain surgeries), physical therapy, leg braces, etc. There have been so many important decisions along the way, and these were often made with limited information. And sometimes as a parent, you choose wrong.

My mission was to raise her as well as I could. Allison didn't realize how much she was loved or why she was loved, but she surely knew she was loved. And I poured so much of myself into her. The result of that effort is that when my co-workers would meet my daughter, they wouldn't say, "She's a lot like you."

Instead, they would say, "She's your clone."

However, having someone copy all your bad traits is a humbling experience. One time when she was seven years old, we were discussing something at dinner. I commented to my wife that Allison thinks she knows everything, which resulted in the following exchange:

Allison: "Father, did you just say that I think I know everything?"

Me: "Yes, I did." (I said sheepishly, thinking I had hurt her feelings)

Allison: "Well, I don't *think* that I know everything—I *do* know everything!"

Today, in 2022, Allison is a healthy, happy, and successful young woman. To respect her privacy, I won't go into much of her adult life, but I can say this: She graduated from a private college in four years with a 3.0 GPA, all while not being able to see or read that well due to an inadequate eyeglass prescription (that has since been corrected). She ran track as best as she could in high school and has run—yes, *run*—in 5K races. That is difficult to do under normal conditions; I can't imagine doing it with a disability.

Allison has a good job and drives to work. She is a voracious reader, (probably due to being read to so much as a baby). She reads about 60 books a year; her best year, she read around 100. We've never tested her IQ, but she is a very intelligent woman.

Raising Allison Ake has been by far the most challenging job I have had in my life. Being the father of a daughter who, at birth, was too stubborn to die when she was supposed to is difficult enough. However, throw in the special needs, high intelligence, and some emotional issues, and it can be highly frustrating. But raising Allison has also been the most rewarding job I have ever had.

I have pushed Allison hard her entire life—part of my promise to raise her the best that I can. While the doctors had set her expectations low, I have set her expectations high. Sometimes, I have pushed her too hard, just as my mother pushed me, and our relationship had suffered as a result.

But life is a tradeoff. You can't have it all. And in this case, I will willingly sacrifice that relationship to ensure my daughter's success. That's the job I pleaded for. That's the job I have done. Sure, I have made mistakes, but I have no regrets.

With Allison, I have had to learn to appreciate what she can do instead of agonizing over what she can't. With her, the glass is forever half full, and my life is richer because of it.

'* Mark Chapter 5

** Psalm 23.4

*** Isaiah 6:5

CHAPTER 4: LIVING TO WIN

Note: This chapter does not include suggestions guaranteed to make you millions of dollars, nor does it feature clever business strategies for "winning" in the corporate world. If that is what you are looking for out of this chapter, then you will be disappointed, especially when you read the final essay. Rather, this chapter explores other ways to "win" in life, ways that can sometimes be deep, heavy stuff.

"Winning" is all in how you define it, and that can influence whether or not you truly "win", and whether you think you are winning or not. The essays here involve having the proper attitude about life, having confidence in your abilities, motivating yourself, and putting yourself first when required.

Following this advice will not make you financially wealthy, but it will lead to an emotionally richer, more fulfilling life. Seize the day and seize your life!

WINNING AT THE GAME OF LIFE

I was taking an early morning walk at the park. I looped around the tennis courts—I often play here, but today, I am just a spectator.

Only one of the ten courts was occupied, and it was odd that it was the farthest one from the parking lot. As I approached that court, I could not see the lone tennis players due to the windscreen on the fence. But I could tell by the constant chatter they were having a competitive match—and a good time, to boot. However, I was stunned when I turned the corner and watched them play.

There were two guys, probably in their late 20's, playing just horrendous, awful tennis. It was apparent they had never had a tennis lesson in their lives. I don't think they had even watched tennis on television, or else they would have at least had some idea of what a proper tennis stroke looked like. They exhibited all the grace and skill of two grandmothers playing badminton. I'm only an intermediate tennis player, but I could have defeated either of them playing left-handed. Really.

However, they *were* evenly matched, which is beneficial for tennis partners. They both hit the ball the same way: horribly. The match was indeed competitive; they were trying hard to win, despite their utter lack of technique. And they were having a blast, laughing hard and frequently at their terrible, errant shots. It was as if they had no idea just how badly they were playing, and they didn't really care. Or maybe they were just laughing at their lack of skill?

As I headed back to the walking track, I smiled as I tried not to laugh out loud at the woeful attempt at "tennis" I had just witnessed.

But then, that irritating inner voice asked a question:

Inner Voice: *"Hey Don, do you have that much fun when you play tennis?"*

Me: "Well, no, I don't."

Inner Voice: *"Why?"*

Me: "I guess sometimes I have trouble controlling my backhand. On certain days, the backhand goes everywhere but in the court. I expect every backhand I hit to be an excellent shot, and when that doesn't happen, I can get irritated and annoyed. My tennis partners no doubt get tired of hearing my constant whining."

Inner Voice: *"So, these two awful tennis players enjoy their time on the court much more than you do?"*

Me: "Uh, yeah..."

Inner Voice: *"Then you may be better at the game of tennis, but those two guys are better at the Game of Life."*

THE GAME OF LIFE

Wouldn't we all be better off if, instead of getting upset at the shots we hit out, we rejoice at the shots we hit in? Perhaps "winning" at the Game of Life is all about managing expectations. We live with high, often impossibly high expectations for our accomplishments, career, income, wealth, children, spouse, other people, coworkers, lifestyle, etc., etc., etc.

How much more satisfying would our lives be if we set our expectations at more realistic levels? Of course, in most situations, we would have to *lower* our expectations. And I don't know how people can set lower, "proper" expectations and still have the motivation to achieve things. However, I am learning. I set high expectations for my first two books and became distressed when they weren't met. I even suffered a panic attack in May 2018 due to this.

But for my third book, I didn't have any expectations at all. I try to delight in each book I sell. I don't even care what the critics say about my book this time—I *know* this is my best writing ever. And I am much happier now than I was during my first two book launches. However, I am still motivated to write and sell more books.

LAUGHING AT YOURSELF

Being able to laugh a lot is a great trait to possess; however, the ability to laugh at *yourself* is precious. Of course, my humor blog attests to the fact that I do that well, but I don't do it as well as those goofy tennis players or my friend, Lynn.

Lynn entertains her Facebook friends with lengthy, hilarious narratives of her foibles and quirks in dealing with her household tasks and crazy life. From the outside, you would not be impressed with Lynn's life. Like all of us, she has made some questionable choices, and in addition, life has dealt her some challenges. However, she doesn't care one bit what you or anyone else thinks about her. You can't judge her because she refuses to put her life on your trial.

Despite everything, Lynn attacks life with gusto. She extracts the maximum enjoyment out of the life she has. Lynn wouldn't trade her life for yours because it doesn't matter. She could extract the same amount of joy out of life, no matter the circumstances. I don't get to see Lynn that often, but she is one of my favorite people. When I'm standing next to her, I feel better due to the positive energy she radiates.

Again, you will not be impressed if you look at her status, job, or life. But the woman is still a winner—a winner at the Game of Life.

WINNING THIS GAME

To conclude, three rules for winning at the Game of Life:

1. Extract as much enjoyment as you can out of everything you do.
2. Set realistic expectations, yet stay motivated.
3. Learn to laugh at yourself more often—don't take yourself or life too seriously!

ARE YOU GOOD ENOUGH?

Because someone, somewhere, needs to hear this ...

In the spring of 2018, Joe Burrows was told he would not be the starting quarterback for Ohio State for the upcoming season.

The message was clear: "You're not good enough."

But Burrows didn't believe them. He transferred to LSU, where he was "good enough" to lead his team to the

2020 National Championship. And, oh yes, in December 2019, the Heisman Trophy voters deemed him not only "good enough", but the best player that season.

Throughout our lives—whether in school, in sports, in our career, in relationships, or pursuing our dreams—we will hear the same message repeated:

"You're not good enough."

Oh, they won't say it that bluntly. "Not good enough" is expressed in many different forms:

"I don't love you anymore."

"We've decided to go another direction."

"You're going to assist Jim on this project."

"You didn't get the job."

"Better luck next time."

"I want a divorce."

"Your contract has not been renewed."

"We're breaking up."

"Your performance didn't measure up."

"You're cut."

"You have failed to meet expectations."

"We're going to have to reject your..."

"We have no interest in your..."

"Don't call us."

"You're fired."

"We've eliminated your position."

We've all heard these, and failure is a part of life. But...

It's not up to other people to decide your value.

YOU DETERMINE IF YOU'RE GOOD ENOUGH!

It is YOUR decision. It is YOUR responsibility. It is YOUR determination.

IT IS YOURS—NOT "THEIRS"!

Many times, as in the case of Joe Burrows, it's not even true when you are deemed insufficient.

Why?

Because people can be:

- Vindictive
- Irrational
- Stupid
- Jealous
- Self-seeking
- Biased
- Ignorant
- Mean
- Just plain wrong

Remember, the people judging you may not have your best interest at heart. Unfortunately, this includes your boss, your friends, your family... even sometimes, your spouse.

Many times, our self-doubt limits us from reaching our potential. We can't let the opinions of others prevent us from pursuing self-actualization.

We can't allow people to stick that "not good enough" label on us like feces. Unfortunately, this fecal matter can adhere to some people their entire lives.

When we let this label stick to us, it paralyzes us with self-doubt and a negative self-image. And once it's on us, it can be hard to wash off. If the comments were made by your parents, boss, partner, or other respected people, it might even take counseling to clean up the mess.

Over the last several months, I have had long, difficult discussions with three friends who were devastated because they were told they weren't "good enough" by their bosses. They all needed affirmation after they were put in unfair situations at work and were basically set up for failure.

It's difficult to overcome being told you're "not good enough", but this is how it's done:

In a 15-month span, between 2015 and 2016, Raheem Mostert was cut by six NFL teams. In effect, he was told he was "not good enough" six times by six different coaches.

Heck, one of those teams was the Cleveland Browns, the worst team in the league at that time. A team that only won one game that entire season. When an awful team says you're not good enough, you must seriously think about quitting. But:

YOU DETERMINE IF YOU'RE GOOD ENOUGH—NOT ANYONE ELSE!

Mostert didn't quit. He thought he was good enough to play in the NFL. He didn't listen to those other six teams. And he was right. As a San Francisco 49'er, he became the first running back in history to run for at least 200 yards and four touchdowns in an NFL Conference Championship in the 2020 NFC championship game.

MAYBE YOU'RE NOT GOOD ENOUGH YET

And there are those instances where *"You're not good enough"* really means "You're not good enough *yet.*"

Except the people giving you the news often don't include the "yet" part because they don't want to help and encourage you. They simply want you to go away. So, hearing those words but not believing them sometimes creates an intense motivation to improve and succeed. Mostert kept the dates he was cut from those six NFL teams listed on his phone as motivation, and no doubt Burrows also felt he had something to prove to himself and others.

Often in life, you are not "good enough" *yet.* No one is born a star. It takes time and hard work to become a master. In the book *Outliers,* Malcolm Gladwell speculates that it takes 10,000 hours of practice to master a skill. Sometimes, we are not "good enough" until we work hard enough to finally get there.

This is not to say you can do anything if you just work hard enough. This is not one of those rah-rah, *"you have the potential to achieve anything"* motivational speeches. This is just deep, heavy stuff, which sometimes means "they" are correct: You are truly *"not good enough"* for the task at hand.

That being said, in most cases, people are not overconfident, they are *under*confident. Psychologists lament the fact that people very often underestimate their potential. Everyone has skills and abilities that they either don't recognize or think are worse than they actually are. Sometimes, we are more than good enough, but we never realize it.

You May Not Be Good Enough

You may, in fact, not be good enough to achieve your goals. We usually can't reach all the success we want, and unless we are exceptional, we have limits.

But the only way to determine if you are *truly* exceptional is to challenge those limits. You've got to test the limits of your capabilities and test them often. Test every day. This means pushing back, sometimes hard, when "they" tell you you're *"not good enough"*.

You may realize at some point that you will not be successful in your chosen pursuit. At that point, it is time to find another challenge. But this is *your* choice and *your* decision.

However, don't let someone who cares nothing—NOTHING—about you divert you from the path you are on. You are the captain of this ship, you steer it where you want it to go. Keep pursuing that dream until you are ready to stop, and don't let the doubters slow you down.

YOU DETERMINE IF YOU'RE GOOD ENOUGH—YOU AND
YOU ALONE!

Raise Your Game This Year

Introduction/Context: I wrote this in the last week of 2021. For the first time during the pandemic, I lived in a "hotspot"—a region of the country with a higher COVID infection rate.

I was becoming fearful again. Events once again were being cancelled. People reverted to sheltering in place. And I could sense the heightened anxiety in everyone around me when I ventured out with my mask.

I had survived a mild case of COVID a year prior, but now, the plague of our age was attacking my inner circle.

A good friend perished the day after Christmas, deflating my post-holiday joy. Then, a childhood friend battled for his life in the hospital. I read the chilling accounts on Facebook as his brother updated us daily. I prayed, I prayed hard, as my friend's condition deteriorated, and he was placed on a ventilator. Thankfully, he survived.

As 2022 began, I was fearful, mentally exhausted, and disappointed at my lack of accomplishments over the past two years. However, I couldn't let those circumstances serve as excuses. It was time to move forward and regain control of my life. No matter what had happened in the past, I needed to raise my game. So, yes, this one was written to myself, and I shared it to encourage others.

I hope this is beneficial to anyone who is trying to recover after hitting a rough patch in life. I wrote this for 2022—read this for whatever year you're in now, or whatever year is just around the corner.

Last year was brutal for many people, and it wasn't

supposed to be that way. After surviving the plague in 2020, we'd hoped 2021 would be a great year. We expected to be able to live and love fully again. That the deaths and infections would cease. That we would return to those good times, the ones we never realized were so good. We just craved some type of normalcy after every routine in our lives was abruptly altered.

We are hopeful creatures. Hope is a great thing: It keeps us moving forward when we don't have the strength to go on. It helps us maintain sanity when our moods are dire. It is the light at the end of our personal darkness. But this year, we never were able to get there. And while hope makes us feel wonderful, when it gets crushed, it only causes more distress.

The plague just hung on, killing hundreds of thousands more—generating fear, sadness, grief, and frustration in us all at once.

Last year brought tremendous sorrow for many people. My friend Harry lamented to me about all the people in his life who were now gone, some from the plague, some from other things. Add the fatalities from the epidemic to the many different causes, and there was one huge pile of death in 2021.

I can count my personal losses this year as well:

My college friend, Graham—virus-related.

My close friend, Dana, who I had helped put her life back together—cancer.

My former work colleague, Mark—virus-related.

Richard, the friendly clerk at my favorite store—heart attack.

Kora, a tremendously sweet, positive woman who led a local author's group—virus-related.

Yes, we must all pass, but these people were all my age or younger.

That gives you pause. It makes you grateful for every breath.

Two years living with the plague has created incredible stress for people. Add in even more pressure—any at all—and bad things happen: the riots, the murders, the crime, the robberies, the arguments, the fights, and so on.

Like many, my mood and outlook have been negatively impacted by the dark clouds of the last two years. I am not treating other people like I should. I'm not thinking as clearly. I am moody and prone to fits of anger. I have lowered my expectations (and not in the good way). I have put my dreams and plans on hold. This change began slowly, and it would have disappeared quickly if the plague had been brief. But after two years, there is a danger these negative traits have burrowed into my soul.

So, join with me here. We have all suffered due to the plague, but now, it is time to break through all the sorrow and weight that has been holding us down. As we enter the new year, it will soon be time to fully live again. It will be time to put away the sorrows and struggles of the past and embrace the future. 2022 (or whatever year you are reading this) is a breakthrough year, and it's time to…

RAISE YOUR GAME.

It's time to treat others better than they deserve. People have been hurting so much. They are moody, angry, rude, argumentative, etc. Realize that and strive to be better in your words and deeds. Imagine you are a nurse walking through a ward of sick people. Deliver the mercy and compassion that these people need. It's time to bring the best "you" to the table and your world.

RAISE YOUR GAME.

Help others when you see they need help. Be the best person you can be because the world has changed—and not for the better. Raise your game and be a better person than you were before the plague. If you don't, you risk holding onto all the negativity weighing you down. This year, be your best person ever because the people around you need it.

RAISE YOUR GAME.

For two years, we have complained about our conditions.

"If it weren't for the plague, I could have achieved..."

"Things would have gone much better, except..."

The plague has weighed us down. The epidemic has frozen us in time. When things break open, there is a risk that we will remain cold and be hesitant to move forward. But we must run hot.

RAISE YOUR GAME.

We must break loose this year. Understand that our efforts in 2020 and 2021 are insufficient for 2022. You have been held down for two years. Now GO! Go fly. Go achieve. Go flourish. It's time to...

RAISE YOUR GAME.

After having trudged through these two awful, terrible years, make 2022 one of the best years of your life.

RAISE YOUR GAME!

CORPORATE LOYALTY IS JUST LIKE BELIEVING IN SANTA CLAUS

Yes, Virginia, your company cares about you...

I regret to inform you that there is no such thing as "corporate* loyalty". It does not exist.

Now, I know many people will argue against this statement. However, I assure you, believing in "corporate loyalty" is the adult equivalent of believing in Santa Claus. Like believing in Santa, believing that your corporation is loyal generates a warm, magical, even Christmas-like feeling. It is so comforting to think that your employer looks out for you and values you much more than your contribution to the firm. It is so uplifting and reassuring; it eliminates many fears, knowing your job is always secure, and that helps you sleep soundly every night.

You can argue by claiming, "Corporate loyalty does too exist, and here's how!" But I will still laugh and shake my head as if you were a five-year-old explaining why Santa Claus is real. Yes, you can believe that corporate loyalty really exists. But like Santa Claus, it doesn't, and I hate to be the one who bursts your bubble.

The purpose of corporations is to generate profit. You are a resource that they use, or employ, to create that profit. Their job is to make money; you are only the means to make that money. As soon as your cost exceeds your benefit, you can be discarded.

The conundrum: You are trying to maximize your salary, which in turn increases your cost. This often means the more money you make, the more expendable your job is.

Now, there is some loyalty within corporations, but it is personnel-based loyalty, not corporate. Usually, the person who hired you is loyal up to a point. However, your job is in immediate danger when your boss leaves the company or transfers out of your department. Your new boss has no loyalty or vested interest in you.

The corporation wants you to believe they are indeed loyal to you because then you will be loyal to them, which is in their best interest. Remember, your parents wanted you to believe in Santa Claus, too.

Now, I am not saying corporations should be loyal or even more "loyal" to their employees—they just aren't. Again, it's that "profit" thing. I won't argue for the existence of corporate loyalty, just as I would not say that Santa should exist. Corporate loyalty just doesn't exist, and you are naïve if you think it does. And unlike Santa, there are costs to believing this myth.

THEN WHAT SHOULD I DO?

If there is no corporate loyalty, then make decisions based on what's right for you, not good for them. Do not sacrifice your health for them. Do not sacrifice your marriage and family for them. Do not sacrifice your soul for them. You owe them your services exchanged for your salary. It is a standard business exchange—nothing more.

Be aware that you are fully responsible for managing your career. Your career path is in your hands. You alone are responsible for your success.

Therefore, always be planning your next step within the corporation or outside of it. Keep developing all the skills you can because these skills are transferrable in ways you can't even imagine. Acquire all the relevant education that is available to you. Focus intently on where you want to go and what you want to do.

Always have a Plan B. A new boss, a buyout, a merger, an internal attack by a coworker, getting blamed for an error you did not make, an unexpected relocation, etc., and you are toast. There is no "loyalty". None.

Continuously be planning your next move. Remember, the company is already playing the game. They are managing you. And they are trying to maximize your value, often at your expense. You'd better learn how to play this game as well, because they certainly are skilled at it. So, if you just pretend the game doesn't exist, then you *literally* get played. Like a skilled chess player, you always need to be thinking several moves ahead.

Build a network of contacts before you need them. You've already heard that networking is essential, but you've ignored it because it seems awkward, takes time, and is unnecessary to your current situation. However, it needs to be part of your Plan B. It is essential to meet and connect with as many people as possible to help you advance in the **next** step in your career plan. By networking, you are investing in yourself, just like in education. It costs you valuable time if you wait until you need a network before building one. It is challenging to drink from the well while you are drilling it.

Networking is also beneficial because it expands your social network. You can become stale if you only interact with coworkers. This lack of diversity binds you to the corporation and results in you absorbing the values of the corporation, which in most cases is deleterious.

APOLOGY

I feel like the parent who has just destroyed the magic of Christmas for their child. Christmas wasn't the same after you learned the truth, was it? But the deep, heavy reality is: Corporate loyalty does not exist. It makes us feel good about our career choices. It provides joy when good things go our way at work. It provides us with the comfort of security, which reduces our anxiety. But it is false security. The most dangerous lies are the ones that we most want to believe. And I am sorry to have to reveal the truth about this one.

WINNING THE GAME

Sometimes, winning in life means looking out for yourself first. Make sure you take responsibility for your own success.

I am defining "corporate" as large companies with more than, say, 100 employees. Company loyalty in smaller organizations can exist in some form.

CHAPTER 5: THOSE WHO HELP YOU GET THERE

No one has gotten to where they are in life without help from others. Sometimes it is obvious, such as when my great-uncle provided my father with the down payment for a house. But many times, the help is so subtle that at the time, you are oblivious to it. There are even cases where you are upset with the very people who are trying to improve your skills.

Here, I detail four essential people who made me an author. Without their help and influence, I would not be an author—thus, you would not be reading this right now.

The last essay is about the only mentor I ever had. Interestingly, he helped me in my side job as a college professor. Sadly, I never had a mentor in my primary profession. My intellect was intimidating to most of my bosses, and I didn't help by being too impersonal in the workplace. Maybe there was someone who wanted to mentor me, but I rejected them because I thought I knew it all.

Receiving and providing help is deep, heavy stuff. My message here is to realize and appreciate it when others try to help you, even if that help comes in the form of criticism. And seek to support and mentor people at every opportunity you can. Even a little encouragement can go a long way if perfectly timed.

BEING HELD TO A HIGHER STANDARD

Almost everyone underestimated my mother's intelligence, even me. It was only after her death that I evaluated all the things she taught me and realized I had been raised by an exceptionally wise woman.

Most people saw a simple housewife who had not made it through her first term at college. But that was due to a nervous condition, not a lack of aptitude. She eventually earned a certification in secretarial skills at a local business college, and she worked as a secretary at Kenmore High School for several years afterward.

Often, it is your coworkers who are the best evaluators of your intelligence because they are privy to your competence and problem-solving skills. So, I believe Miss Jameson, an English teacher at Kenmore, was one of the few people who knew my mother's true intellectual capacity.

Therefore, when Betty Ake's son appeared in Miss Jameson's English Composition class seventeen years after Betty's retirement, she had high expectations about the kid's ability and potential. Yes, Betty Ake's boy had to be a great writer, didn't he? And if he wasn't, didn't Miss Jameson have the responsibility to make him one?

My expectations going into the class, however, were much lower. I had gotten closed out of the college prep English class that term and had to take the much easier English Composition class instead. And I was not impressed with this older teacher who I have described in my humor book *Turkey Terror At My Door!* as resembling a *"fireplug in an unfashionable flowery dress"*. I planned to cruise effortlessly though this class and pick up an easy "A".

Miss Jameson had other ideas. She was going to hold me to a much higher standard. My first composition, which I put minimal effort in, was returned to me covered in red ink with a big letter "C" at the top of the page. Meanwhile, other students received "B" grades for essays not as good as mine.

I screamed, "Unfair!" I protested vehemently to Miss Jameson after class. I complained so much to my mother that she actually visited her old friend at the school to discuss this particular injustice.

But to my disbelief, the grade stood.

I was scared out of my mind that I might get a "C" or worse in this supposedly "easy" class. I had to work harder than I had in any prior writing class (and arguably, harder than I would have worked in that elite English class) to meet an unusually high—and what I considered unfair—standard. In order to survive, among other things, I had to learn to rewrite and edit, two skills which any proficient writer must master. Yes,

I was motivated by fear, but I was highly motivated. Miss Jameson was fully aware of what she was doing, but I was clueless for over forty years.

I came out of that class a much better writer than when I went in, even if I only earned a "B" as my final grade. That, my friends, is one exceptional teacher.

For years, I resented Miss Jameson's treatment of me. She would have ranked high on my list of worst high school teachers. I hated my time in her class, and that feeling persisted for years.

It was only after reading about Miss Jameson's death that I realized what she truly did for me and why. Someone who sees your potential and helps you develop it is not only an exemplary teacher but a great person. The fact that she did this despite how I felt about her makes her extra special.

Miss Jameson made me a better writer whether I wanted to be one or not. For that, I am very grateful.

She Saw Talent I Didn't Know I Had

Some decisions are so simple and impulsive, yet they can turn out to have tremendous implications in the long run. One casual choice I made when I was 17 years old determined the course of the rest of my life. In fact, you would not be reading this except for that seemingly unimportant decision.

In May 1975, I had to choose my courses for the final year of high school. I'm sure my mother had guided my selections in the past to ensure I was on track to graduate. However, the senior year choices were easy: select the senior-level college prep courses and be done. But I still had to choose one more elective class.

While most of my classmates had no doubt picked an easy, fun class, I chose Journalism.

My parents were dedicated newspaper readers, subscribing to two daily papers. By high school, I was reading all of one paper and part of the second and thus had a strong interest in journalism; therefore, I knew that class would be fun for me.

However, the class atmosphere was different. All the students there were underclassmen taking the class because it was considered the easiest class to take for an English requirement. These students were not "Honor Society" types. If you could write complete sentences about stuff you knew, you could pull a "C" grade. Before one of the first classes, the dude next to me wanted to engage in a conversation about the quality of weed he had smoked that weekend. I just nodded with a smile, said, "That's nice," and hoped he would shut up.

The class was taught by one Margaret Maher. She was the perfect teacher for this class of hooligans. She was very patient and flexible, but her military background enabled her to command respect and restore order quickly if necessary. She made sure everyone benefited from the class whether they wanted to or not.

But in this gang of burnouts, there was one student who was soaking up everything, enthralled by learning how newspaper articles were created. I think you can guess who that one student was.

One day, Mrs. Maher announced that she was looking for people who wanted to write for the school newspaper, *The Cardinal*. I probably signed up for my future career as an author that day as well. That was "day one" of becoming a writer.

My first articles were about sports, since that was an interest of mine. But then, there was that fateful day in December, detailed in my book *Turkey Terror At My Door!*, when Mrs. Maher saw a humor writer in her midst. Before I had written even a single joke or funny story, she saw potential. This is what mentors, helpers, and outstanding educators do.

She realized I had two talents—humor and writing—and decided to combine them. She ordered me to write my first humor column over Christmas break, used her authority to have it published, and encouraged me to do more. She struck the match, lit the fuse, and stood back, launching my writing career.

The writing skills I developed in this class also contributed to success in my business career. I have written newsletters, as well as many important reports and analyses over the years.

First, I continued to write at The University of Akron, detailed in the following essays. And eventually, after that, four books, including this one. All because of one person who told me to "write down some of those jokes, and we will print them in the newspaper."

Mrs. Maher probably had the most influence on my life, more than anyone else.

Oh, and that simple check mark choosing journalism as an elective? Not only leading to the successes listed above, but also leading to my marriage: I met my future wife on campus as a direct result of writing for The University of Akron *Buchtelite*. My wife-to-be worked on the yearbook staff, whose office was right across the hall from the newspaper. So, that simple observation and challenge from Mrs. Maher influenced my life in many ways and as you read this, that influence continues.

KIND WORDS – PERFECTLY TIMED

My heart raced when I arrived on campus that spring morning in 1977. My first standard humor piece, byline and all, was scheduled to run in the Friday edition of The University of Akron *Buchtelite*. My hands shook as I grabbed a copy by the door and headed for Speech class.

The paper had published several of my news and sports articles my freshman year, but this was the first humor column that was in the spirit of my high school writing. There had also been a couple of humorous feature pieces, but this was a test to see how my brand of humor played to the college crowd.

This article was important to me. It had been rewritten numerous times. It had made it through the review process with minimal efforts. Yes, this was a big day for me.

I sat down, whipped open the paper, and there it was on Page 5.

There is this surge a writer gets when they see their name in print. It's the same today when I get quoted in my day job by the business press. It is further intensified when that "business press" is the *Wall Street Journal* or *Reuters*.

Boom! Look at that! My first college humor column. Someone had made it to what they perceived as the "big time". It was one step up an unimaginably tall ladder. There was that special feeling, the adrenaline rush, with all those wonderful endorphins. Everyone on campus would be reading my masterpiece today.

But then, there was the realization that no other student in the room was reading the *Buchtelite*. And everyone was visible to me because in this speech classroom, the desks were placed along the walls facing the open middle.

This was devastating. The students had nothing better to do than read a free copy of the campus paper while waiting for their first class to start. But they had walked right past the stack of newspapers in the lobby and were content to sit there like mindless zombies, waiting for class to begin.

A massive rush of self-pity replaced that exhilaration. So much time and effort had been put into that article! It was well-written and funny! I received no pay for this, and the time spent writing it could have been spent studying. And now it seemed like such a waste of time and effort.

Now, the pity party was in full force. I instantly decide this would be the last humor piece I would ever write for the *Buchtelite*. I quit! I'm done! The decision is final!

Most often, these impulsive, emotionally-charged decisions are reversed after I calm down and rationality returns. However, not always. Sometimes, those decisions stick and remain forever. But on that day, my quick decision to stop writing humor never had a chance.

As the disappointment raged on, a cute young woman named Melissa, who knew me from a previous class, walked over to me from across the classroom.

"I really liked your article in the paper today. It made me laugh," she said.

"Thank you," I muttered.

I sat there mesmerized while Melissa returned to her seat. She must have read my column before coming to class.

And then, creativity—with a dash of young man hormones—jolted me right out of that funk. Immediately, my mind began searching for the topic for my next humor piece. How could it not? *Melissa* liked it! Did I mention her cuteness?

Could my writing career have ended that day in that classroom, had Melissa not complimented me? Maybe. But it didn't. Regardless, I owe Melissa a great debt of gratitude for speaking words of encouragement at the very moment I needed to hear them.

So, the lesson here is: Be sure to encourage others every opportunity you get. Like Melissa's, your words may have a tremendous positive impact that you never see.

What about the problem with students not reading the *Buchtelite*? Truth be told, there was really nothing interesting or compelling in it. It was dry and boring. But that was about to change, as you will read in the next essay.

The following year, a sophomore would launch a weekly humor column so popular that many students actually looked forward to reading the *Buchtelite* every Friday.

And this writer went on to... well, you know.

Editor Jane Was a Big Pain

A few weeks after arriving on The University of Akron campus in the fall of 1976, I volunteered to write for the student newspaper. My goal was to continue to write humor and duplicate the success I had in high school.

Few students read the *Buchtelite* (the name being a holdover from when the school was known as Buchtel College). Akron U was a commuter school operating in the center of town. It was one of the most boring campuses in the country. There was little of significance for the newspaper to report on, and when there was, most of the students didn't care. Many referred to the school as "Apathy U".

I started off writing news, sports, and a couple of feature articles. I convinced the Feature Editor to let me write some humor pieces. I knew I had to catch the readers' attention, so these early efforts were outrageous and shocking, sort of like the strategy employed by Howard Stern. They were published only because they weren't dull, and the *Buchtelite* had nothing better to print. If these same articles were published today (first of all, they wouldn't dare), I would be immediately expelled. If I ran for political office today, these *awful*, politically incorrect essays would make headlines.

Before my sophomore year, I marched up to the *Buchtelite* office and pitched my idea to write a weekly humor column called "Ake's Pains".

I was brash. I was outrageous. I was filled with all the naïve bravado of a 19-year-old guy. There is no way they should have ever agreed to this.

But Editor Jane said, "Sure, let's try it!"

I'm not sure if she actually liked the idea or she just needed to fill space on the editorial page once a week.

Therefore, Jane became my first real editor. And as a writer, I hate editors. Because editors take your perfect writing, mark it up, and change things until your work becomes less than perfect. And make no mistake, my writing was perfect—*absolutely perfect*—because I was a 19-year-old college student, and I thought I knew everything.

Oh, how I hated Editor Jane. Now, only as an editor, mind you. Regular Jane was sweet, pleasant, intelligent, funny, and also... cute! Nothing to dislike there.

But I always became agitated during our weekly closed-door (so nobody could hear the yelling) meetings when we reviewed my upcoming column.

Most of the editing meetings went like this:

Editor Jane: You can't say this part. It is offensive.

Me: But that's what makes it funny!

Editor Jane: And this part needs totally rewritten to make it less outrageous.

Me: But that's the best part of the whole column!

Editor Jane: And this paragraph is out!

Me: Noooooooooooooooooooooooooo!

I would walk out of those meetings agitated, believing Editor Jane had ruined my masterpiece. But regardless of her hatchet jobs, the column was a big hit. The students loved my satirical wit and how I made fun of all the stupid stuff on campus. They especially enjoyed it when I stuck it to "The Man".

However, "The Man"—that being the university administration—was much less amused by my rants. I could imagine the bigwigs getting all red-faced when the *Buchtelite* hit campus Friday morning. To them, I was not funny at all. I was a scourge, and they took offense at my jabs.

For example, students had discovered cockroaches in one of the dorms—a very embarrassing situation for the administration. The following week, I wrote that the biggest event on campus was the cockroach races being held in West Haven Dorm, with the winner being Secretari-roach. *(You old-timers will get the joke!)*

At the time, I hated Editor Jane and how I thought she diluted my humor. However, when I look back, I realize that Editor Jane had played a critical part in my progression from a writer to an author. I would not have ever written three books if it was not for the hated Editor Jane.

Editor Jane was able to skillfully edit my work so that students still thoroughly enjoyed it and found it humorous, yet it was not so outrageous that the administration shut me down. And I'm sure there were phone calls from the higher-ups telling her that enough was enough, that the Ake guy was a real pain and needed to be silenced. But Editor Jane never buckled to the pressure.

Editor Jane had my best interest at heart. She coached me, mentored me, improved my writing, and helped me. She never outright rejected a column. She never told me to "tone it down". She just let me be me, and then was so skilled at polishing those literal sophomoric expressions into fantastic columns. She let me protest loudly, but she kept me around. She threaded that needle perfectly.

She gave me an opportunity that I didn't deserve and made me a success at that critical point in my literary career. And for all that, I hated her. I took her for granted. I viewed the situation from the selfish perspective of an immature college guy with no appreciation at all for how much she was helping me.

Because of Editor Jane, I wrote columns for three years in college, experimenting with different styles my senior year. I thought "Ake's Pains" was done when I graduated. But 31 years later, "Ake's Pains" was resurrected as a humor blog and was the catalyst for all three of my humor books.

We need to appreciate those people who are helping us now and have helped us in the past, and we need to express that appreciation to them. More importantly, we also need to be the one who helps others along the way because we have no idea how our efforts may inspire someone to achieve greatness.

FROM RIDICULOUS TO RIDICULOUSLY CORRECT

Everyone in the marketing program at The University of Akron raved about Dr. George Prough. However, after declaring my major as a sophomore, I would have to wait two years before I was finally able to take his Promotional Strategies course my last semester on campus.

From the first class, I realized all the praise was warranted: Dr. Prough's teaching style was distinct, unique, and exceptional. He didn't lecture on "theory"— he expected you to read that stuff in the textbook and come to class prepared. What he lectured about were real-life examples and applications that cemented those theories in your brain.

And then, there was the outrageous humor, but it wasn't meant to entertain. The humor was used as an important teaching tool, closely related to the topics to make sure we understood and, more importantly, remembered them.

Dr. Prough's class was a fast-moving, free-wheeling joyride through the world of marketing, and to say I flourished under this teaching style was an understatement. Dr. Prough was my best instructor ever by far. It was like a mind-meld. I thoroughly soaked up everything contained in this course, and my grades were stellar. I never was bored in his class and was disappointed when the bell rang.

That being said, though, I don't think I spoke up much the whole semester. I didn't ask questions since I understood everything the first time. I sat quietly in the last row and never spoke to Dr. Prough before, after, or outside of class. I didn't think he even knew my name.

An Outrageous Statement

However, that was far from the case. There were only a few students left in the room as I finished my essay-question final exam in Promotional Strategies. Most of the remaining students were clustered on the left side of the room, so I walked down the right aisle to turn in my exam booklet. Dr. Prough got up from his chair and met me before I turned the corner. I handed him my test.

"You should be a marketing professor," he said.

I nodded and said, "Thank you."

But it was one of the most outrageous statements anyone had ever said to me. A marketing professor? That was laughable! It wasn't even in the range of possibilities. I was vigorously job-hunting and was going to be married in a few months. And why would he say that after me taking one course? We had never even had a conversation! He really didn't know that much about me. It was pure kooky talk. I immediately rejected the advice as pure folly. But I still remembered that moment, only because it was so bizarre.

The Reconnection

I graduated, started my career, went to graduate school, and otherwise lived my life.

Several years later, the business college started a program called "Professor for a Day", where graduates were invited back to campus to teach a class. I participated a couple times and enjoyed it.

The third time I signed up, I received a call from the administrator asking if I would be interested in teaching Dr. Prough's class. This, to me, was an honor.

I did such a good job teaching his class the first time that he always requested me for future events. I taught his class for "Professor for a Day" for years, and we'd become quite the impressive team. And now, I was able to spend time with him—discussing marketing, career, and life—before and after the class. We became good friends.

Whenever I taught Dr. Prough's class, I would do short segments on real-life examples applied to marketing principles. After class, we would discuss my presentation, and he would point out which segments worked best. I didn't realize it at the time, but I was being mentored. The next time I taught, I would repeat the good examples and add some new ones. Over time, I had an outstanding presentation.

The odd thing is: He never criticized any of the weak examples. He just praised the good stuff.

Make of that what you will.

THE NEXT STEP

Around 2003, Indiana Wesleyan University opened a Cleveland campus and recruited for adjunct business faculty. You didn't need previous teaching experience, but you had to survive a challenging screening process. The final step was a 10-minute teaching presentation in front of the selection committee as well as every other person competing for a teaching position. This was done in a jam-packed conference room, and to this day, it was the most high-pressure presentation I have ever done.

But little did I know, I had been preparing for this moment for years—with Dr. Prough's guidance. I took the best segment from "Professor for a Day", expanded it to 10 minutes, and then delivered it flawlessly under pressure.

Almost all the other candidates had had previous college teaching experience, but the campus dean told me later that my presentation was the best one that night.

HEY, I'M A PROFESSOR!

Now I was adjunct faculty, but I was still inexperienced and unproven. Therefore, you start at the bottom. They gave me the course that nobody wants to teach: Basic Economics at the associate degree level. Most students in the associate program have already started their business careers and are taking college classes for the first time. They work all day, grab something to eat, and then head to my class. Meanwhile, it was my job to teach them basic economics from 6 to 10 p.m.

I quickly realized that I couldn't lecture on economics for four hours at night without the students fading out. So, I didn't teach theories. I started with real-life examples that the students were familiar with, and I then extruded the theories from the examples. It wasn't a lecture; it was a quick-moving presentation with a lot of humor mixed in—not for entertainment purposes, but to reinforce the concepts. There were also videos and projects provided by the university to break up class time.

And it worked! The students who expected economics to be difficult and boring ended up loving the class. One student labeled it "stand-up economics", since I always told the class I had done stand-up comedy at one time. And best of all, they were learning economics. They were *getting it*.

My first five-week course went well. I was making the long drive home after the second night of my second course, energized because things had just gone so well.

Wow! I thought to myself. *You are good at this, and you caught on very quickly. You even have a style! Where did that come from? What does it remind you of?*

And then, of course, the epiphany. It wasn't "my" style after all—it was my version of Dr. George Prough's! I was unconsciously imitating the best professor I had ever known. Oh, and it worked so well!

ABSURD? – NO, ABSURDLY BRILLIANT

I received high marks from the student reviews in my economics classes. Having proven myself, they asked me to teach a bachelor's marketing class. I felt like a minor leaguer getting called to join the major leagues. Yes, I was a marketing professor—26 years after Dr. Prough's proclamation. The statement that I considered absurd… was actually absurdly brilliant. The man had been able to ascertain my destiny by evaluating just a small sample of my classwork, and had been a mere 26 years ahead of me.

When my marketing textbook arrived at my house, I unwrapped it like a kid at Christmas. Then, I held the book in both hands like it was a sacred scroll. I was so mesmerized by it that I read all the introduction pages that no one ever reads.

But I stopped when it said the book was "exceptional" because it had been reviewed by the top marketing professors in the country, listing all their names and universities.

Oh yeah? All the top profs, huh? We'll see about that.

And I turned the pages, searching for one name.

And there it was.

"Dr. George Prough – The University of Akron".

My ascent to marketing professor should have led to a joyous celebration with Dr. Prough, one where we would share some drinks, share some laughs, and I would remind him about his advice given 26 years earlier.

But sadly, there was no celebration. About this time, Dr. Prough was stricken with Parkinson's Disease and had to stop teaching. I did, however, send him a letter thanking him for everything.

The last I saw Dr. Prough was at a university breakfast in 2011. He was confined to a wheelchair, and there was a large group of people gathered around him.

After the university president had greeted Dr. Prough, I grabbed his shoulder, pointed at Dr. Prough, and said, "The best. The absolute best," and he nodded in agreement.

I then said what was basically hello and goodbye to my mentor and friend. Dr. Prough passed away a year and a half later. I attended the funeral.

I wanted to be a full-time marketing professor. I seriously investigated it three different times, but I just couldn't make the personal economics work. I guess the time to have planned this move was maybe, say, 26 years ago?

Now, the whole purpose of this story is to show that the idea of mentoring and being mentored is so beneficial and needed. I could have written ten whole pages of lectures on "mentoring", but I chose instead to show you instead of telling you. I think I learned that from Dr. Prough.

Therefore, I said all that to say this:

If you are at the later stages of your career, where you are confident enough that you don't need to compete with everyone: share your knowledge about life, skills, philosophy, business, and "life hacks" with anyone who will listen. And if someone realizes the value in your wisdom, mentor them.

Likewise, you younger folk, especially those who think they know it all: listen to the older guys and women. It can keep you from making so many stupid mistakes. It can also help you achieve more in your career, much faster. So, if you find someone who is willing to invest in you as a mentor, seize the opportunity.

CHAPTER 6:
BUILDING AND GROWING PERSONAL RELATIONSHIPS

Personal relationships are essential to a happy, healthy life. There have been many studies done on the benefits of having a strong network of friends as well as support groups.

This chapter is a collection of essays about strengthening bonds and helping people along as they help you. Many people don't understand what being a good friend is. I know this because most people do it wrong, and good people are hurt because of it.

In this chapter, we look at how we can be the best friends we can possibly be. In order to do that, we need to be encouraging, caring, and to intercede when necessary. There is also the cold reality that not every close associate is indeed your friend.

If you find anything that helps you in this chapter, consider me your friend.

NOBODY'S PERFECT – SO STOP EXPECTING THEM TO BE

Recently, I had to replace my old clock radio. Yes, I'm a "Boomer", so I use a clock radio rather than my phone alarm to wake myself up every morning.

I'm glad my old radio finally died because I hated it. It was difficult to tune, and I had to adjust it frequently because the controls were poorly positioned. Resetting the time was complicated and could never be done without reading the instructions. And on top of that, the battery backup mechanism was busted.

However, my new clock radio has many great, convenient features: The radio is easy to tune and has a digital display. I can also set the time and alarms easily and quickly. It has dual alarms—one for weekdays and one for weekends—which I need. It even has two USB ports for charging my devices overnight.

This new clock radio is tremendously superior to my old one, except for one glaring deficiency: It doesn't keep time very well. It is a clock radio that is great in every aspect except that "clock" part, one of its two core functions. At least it is easy to reset, which I now do often.

And in contemplating the absurdity of this irony, I realize the clock radio suffers from the same fate as us humans: No one is proficient in everything. Everyone has weaknesses, blind spots, deficiencies, and Achilles' Heels. There are imperfections in every one of us.

When the molecules are blended into our DNA, some abilities are in short supply, while others may be lacking altogether. This results in people such as mathematical geniuses who are incapable of driving a car. Some politicians are extraordinary problem-solvers who lack empathy for the people they are elected to serve. In my case, I can make sense of complex data, seeing how all the pieces fit together. However, if I must put anything tangible together, even a simple assembly, those "pieces-parts" suddenly become impossible for me to connect. I am a master of the theoretical but helpless in the physical realm. You may be like any of these examples, the opposite of these examples, or a different combination of strengths and deficiencies altogether. The point is that some parts of your brain are exceptional; other parts are barely proficient.

This is why I believe we are all "mentally ill" to some extent. Some only slightly, and some in harmless areas that don't matter much. Regardless, I contend that *no one* has a perfect brain (you will see why in a moment), and therefore, everyone has a brain that "malfunctions" somehow. Accepting this about ourselves and others will bring us closer together and help us work through each other's "malfunctions".

You would think that in all the billions of people who have ever lived, there would be at least one case where, by random chance, the DNA clicked perfectly together to produce the perfect person. However, it never has and probably never will. Yes, there is that notable exception, but I'm not sure what that "not totally human" DNA looks like under a microscope.

But even though we know the perfect person doesn't exist (and probably won't), we still expect our fellow human beings to be perfect. We readily acknowledge that we ourselves have faults and weaknesses, yet we get frustrated when people behave stupidly or fail to perform to our standards.

We tend to overvalue our proficiencies simply because we are good at those things, and we undervalue traits that we deem less important (For example, you don't really appreciate the skills of a plumber until your toilet breaks). Thus, we get highly agitated with someone when they make a stupid blunder doing something in which we consider ourselves to be proficient ("How could they possibly mess that up?!"). However, we still identify with and show empathy to people making the same mistakes that we do.

An important aspect of wisdom gained from experience is to know your strengths and your weaknesses. This knowledge permits you to avoid failures and admire those with those skills which you lack. If you don't already know your strengths and weaknesses, it's time for some self-reflection (There are self-assessment tests you can take online).

I don't know why we expect anyone to be perfect. Either there is some strange evolutionary benefit of having high expectations (maybe we killed off all those who frustrated us too much), or we were created as imperfect beings by a perfect being. The latter may explain where our concept of "perfect" originated.

When we don't expect perfection from other people, we aren't as irritated and judgmental when they fall short.

It also helps us in our personal relationships with people different than ourselves.

The art of making good friends centers around accepting people as they are, including their faults. This vital trait enables you to expand your circle of friends and experience a diversity of thought and life experiences. Part of being a good friend is to help others through their weakness, especially if you have a strength in that area. Sometimes, the friendships you make with people who are different from you become the strongest, longest-lasting relationships in your life.

Key Thought: Do not expect other people to be perfect because you are not perfect.

Just as people irritate you because they are different, consider that some people may be irritated by you just as much. For example, intelligent people can be frustrated by the actions of the less intelligent, and the less intelligent get annoyed when the "eggheads" can't explain things in simpler terms and get upset over trivial matters.

But the challenge now is to learn how to be more tolerant of others when they fail, especially in areas where we excel. This is difficult when that failure or mistake costs us time, money, or something else valuable to us. However, if we can offer our strengths to help others' weaknesses and receive that same assistance with our own struggles, life would be so much better.

However, being forgiving, tolerant, and compassionate does not come naturally to us because ... we are not perfect.

BE THEIR FRIEND - IF ONLY FOR TODAY

All your life you've encountered them: older people making the effort to converse with you at random. Sometimes, they even say stupid stuff that you really don't understand.

And this tendency has irritated you. As you stand behind them at the grocery store, post office, or bank, they are just jabbering away at the clerk or cashier about any mundane topic, and you can't wait for them to shut up and move on.

But once you reach a certain age, you begin to understand what's going on: These people are lonely and isolated. They want human interaction. They need to talk to anyone about anything. They are so desperate for conversation that they will just blurt out things that don't make sense, hoping you will answer them.

As you age, you become less mobile, and your circle of friends tightens due to isolation and expiration. When my mother died, I went through her paper address book to see who she might have wanted to be notified. The pages were filled with red "X"s; I stopped halfway through because it was so depressing.

It is bittersweet to outlive your friends.

Given these reasons, an older person's need for human contact increases. Their "world" shrinks, beyond their control more often than not, and the "little things" become magnified. That conversation at the grocery store, which you see as an inconvenience, may be the highlight of their day. A brief and seemingly inconsequential chat could be the difference between them feeling loved or feeling alone in the world.

I so much regret all the times I have declined talking to an elderly person. My natural tendency is not to interact with strangers about trivial matters, but that is a selfish response.

You could even include the lonely people at work who try to have personal conversations about anything. Find the time to talk with them.

These people need contact. They need conversation. Please talk to them when they try to engage you. Be patient when they are talking to other people. Be their friend, if only for today.

YOU HAVE FEWER FRIENDS THAN YOU THINK

Your circle of friends is much smaller than you think it is.

Yes, you have many people who associate with you. Maybe you have thousands of "friends" and contacts on social media. But in reality—cold reality—your *true* friends are few. You find out who is really on your team when you get knocked down or even hit bottom. Some people will kick you, most will avoid you, but a select few will reach down and help pull you up. Another acid test for friendships is asking for something that requires time or money. And sadly, many friendships are not even worth $10.

No, when you ask for help, the "acquaintances" and "associates" scatter like flies or go "radio silent". Indeed, in times of struggle, you find who your true friends are.

LOYAL TO A FAULT

Loyalty is a concept not shared equally among individuals.

People who are "loyal to a fault" expect the same level of commitment from people they consider friends. Unfortunately, disloyal people are willing to discard any relationship, even a "lifelong" friendship, as easily as flicking away an irritating bug when it no longer benefits them. Sometimes, as soon as the relationship hits a stress point or you ask for any level of commitment, you find out there had never really been a friendship at all, and if a loyal person finds themselves in this situation, it can feel like getting hit with a ton of bricks.

The loyal person wonders what they did to cause the relationship to end, followed up by the inevitable, "What's wrong with me?". They will impulsively try to restore what they thought was a good friendship: They will apologize. They will make excuses for the other person. They may even try to change their behavior to make it work. But this effort will inevitably fail. When that happens, the loyal person will be deeply hurt, sometimes beating themselves up and blaming themselves for years.

But while you are doing that, the other person has forgotten all about you. They may have even forgotten your name.

What you must realize, in this situation, is that the friendship was always one-sided. There is nothing wrong with you, except that you are too loyal. And as with everything in life, even though loyalty is a good trait, there is a price to pay for having too much of it. Just like being "too" good, "too" nice, "too" trusting, "too" patient ....

The real problem here is with the other person. There is something wrong with *them*, not you. There is nothing you could have done to save this relationship because there never really was one to begin with. You thought they were your friend, but they never considered you a friend. As soon as you no longer had any value to them, you were quickly disposed of.

So you are giving value to someone who deserves no value. The person literally is "not worth it". Trying to salvage friendships like these is like trying to hug the air. It is a futile effort. Yes, you made a poor value judgment, but now, it is time to reevaluate.

IT STILL HURTS, THOUGH.

It's always painful for the "loyalists" when a friendship evaporates. And sometimes, people you liked and trusted can suddenly become mean, conniving backstabbers with no warning whatsoever.

It's even more frustrating at work. People in the office will smile to your face and laugh with you one minute, then throw you under the bus not a moment later. There is so much betrayal in the business world that being a "Judas" is often an unspoken part of the job description.

You don't even know who your *best* friends are at work. I was at a company for many years, and I thought I had made several strong friendships that would last a lifetime. However, many of my closest "friends"—my *best* work friends—still "ghost" me to this day.

One time, I had to get in touch with one of these "*best* work friends" regarding a business issue with my first book. He didn't return my voicemails; he didn't return my emails. Finally, I mailed a letter explaining what I needed. Crickets. This is hurtful, but I need to let this go and stop hugging the air.

Most of the time, we can't put a value on our friendships. However, a few years ago, a person I thought was a friend sold me out for a mere $50. If a friendship is not worth $50 to you, you are not a "friend"—you are a mere acquaintance. The fact that I am writing about this one after all this time indicates that I am still hugging that air.

It's All About Value

We make so many value judgments that we don't evaluate which ones are faulty. Once you spot the sell-outs, the hangers-on, and the passive-aggressors, don't try to salvage the relationships. Don't invest anything more in them. Cut them loose.

What you must do is find the people in your "inner circle". Identify those who are on your team. And then nurture, support, help, and invest in those people with everything you have. Because it is these people who will support and help you when you need it most.

Support me, and I will support you. It is such a simple concept, and yet few people get it.

Determine who is worthy of your investment, and then invest in them. If you are on my team, there are benefits to being on my team.

A WARNING

Be aware: Not everyone you think is a "friend" is really your friend. Most are acquaintances, and sadly, some are even your enemies (or at the very least, they find some perverse pleasure when you fail). I wish it didn't have to be that way, but it is one of many human frailties in this game of life.

Go For It!

I first met Shantelle at an authors' fair a few years ago. She impressed me as an intelligent, beautiful young woman. Her hair was a work of art, featuring many complicated long braids. I added her to the email list for my authors' group, but she never attended.

Two years later, I see three women together at a networking event. I introduce myself to the first two, but when I turn to the third one, she smiles broadly and starts to giggle.

"Oh, Don! You know who I am. We've met before."

I study her intently, but I have no clue who she is.

"I'm Shantelle!" she exclaims as the giggling resumes.

Of course, I'm embarrassed, believing that my fading memory has failed me again. I apologize profusely, glad that she is amused and not offended by my omission.

I strike up a conversation with her and her friends when it suddenly hits me why I failed to recognize her.

"Wait! Your hair! Your hair is completely different! That's why I didn't recognize you!" I blurt out, interrupting the discussion.

Now, the giggles are replaced by hearty laughter by all the women.

"Yes, it's very different from when we first met," she admits.

We became Facebook friends soon afterward, which hopefully helps my memory when I see Shantelle the next time. It was quickly apparent by Shantelle's posts that her hair is one of her hobbies. She changes her hairstyle frequently. However, regardless of the various styles, there is one constant: In every photo, she is gorgeous.

I messaged her: *Have you ever thought about doing some modeling?*

Her response: *People tell me that all the time, lol, but I've never pursued it.*

I've encouraged Shantelle to put together a portfolio and submit it to an agency. I hope that someday she does, because:

YOU NEED TO PURSUE YOUR DREAMS!

You need to have the courage to try new things to see how high you are meant to fly. And you can't do that standing on the ground.

People don't try because they are afraid to fail. But you still get more out of life when you fail often and when you fail big than when you "don't fail at all".

This sounds counterintuitive, but you must go for it. No one succeeds at anything on their first attempt. Often, the most accomplished people are the stubborn ones— or even the stupid ones—who try and fail repeatedly.

Yes, there is a risk of failure. However, there is also a risk of not trying. It is called "regret", and regrets are lousy because they tend to be persistent and difficult to shake.

In encouraging people to go for it, we can reduce the amount of regrets. We can forget and get beyond our failures, but we will roll those regrets over and over. Some regrets stay with us for life.

I have a list of failures, things I tried that never worked out. I also have a list of regrets. But someday, when I'm sitting in a nursing home contemplating my life, I'm not going to be saddened by my failures, and more importantly, there will be fewer regrets.

YOU HAVE TO GO FOR IT – AND KEEP GOING FOR IT!

Most people stop because failure hurts. Failures generate pain, which is burdensome because your own actions created it. However, this life is a long-distance race.

All long-distance runners come to the point in the race where the pain reaches its apex. At that point, you can quickly alleviate the pain by just stopping. Quit the race. Stop the pain. But the winners know they must finish the race, which means running *through* the pain. We are better off for those "winners", those high achievers who wouldn't have achieved their goals and made the world a better place unless they tried and failed at the beginning.

THE RESPONSIBILITY YOU HAVE AS A FRIEND

Friendship plays a huge role in what people can achieve. As a friend, you should always look for exceptional traits in others and encourage them to "go for it!"

Let's say your friend is repeatedly failing in their current line of work. You see they are not a good fit for the job they have now, but they have traits and skills that are better applicable elsewhere. Just the simple advice, "Have you ever thought about doing _____?" could change a person's life.

Your other responsibility as a friend is to give support when your friends try and fail. Failure hurts, but it stings more when you fail alone. Try to guide them through it as much as you can. Encourage them to keep moving forward if appropriate. Invite them out for coffee or lunch, and then just sit back and listen. That's what friends do. That's what friends are for.

YOU NEED TO PURSUE YOUR DREAMS. YOU NEED TO TRY!

If you are young, you need to pursue these dreams with passion. If you are older and winding down your life, you need to encourage the younger people in your "sphere of influence" to pursue their dreams.

I hope Shantelle follows my advice and sends her portfolio to an agency to see what happens. Probably nothing will, but she won't know until she tries.

LISTEN TO THOSE VOICES

Yes, we need to pursue our dreams, but which dreams are worthy of chasing?

When I suggested that Shantelle consider modeling, her response was literally, "I get that a lot."

So numerous people are presenting Shantelle with the same idea. What should she do? People are always offering us ideas or suggestions about various things. How do we tell which ones are valid?

These ideas/suggestions fall into three categories:

- Really Good No-Brainers

  These are excellent ideas that you know are
  winners the moment they hit your ears.
  Sometimes, they are so obvious that you can't
  believe you never thought of that. You
  enthusiastically thank the person for their
  wisdom and take the recommended action as
  soon as possible.

- Really Bad No-Brainers

  These are bad ideas. Sometimes, *really* bad
  ideas that will most likely fail miserably with
  possibly harmful consequences. The person
  offering them either doesn't understand the
  situation or may be a bit dim-witted. You nod,
  smile, say, "That's interesting," and hope the
  subject never comes up again.

- The Unknowns/Possibles

  These ideas could be good or could be bad. You
  may have considered them in the past. You may
  have even tried them previously with little
  success. These ideas tend to be more complex
  and may take extra time, effort, or resources to
  implement. You can't decide if you should try
  the idea because it is a question of evaluating
  the risks versus the rewards.

MAKING DECISIONS ABOUT THE UNKNOWNS

We tend to automatically dismiss the "Unknowns" because we instinctively focus on the risks rather than the rewards. We focus on the negative outcomes and why the idea will not work.

"I could try that, but I would need to this, this, and this, and it probably wouldn't work."

Therefore, the first time the idea is suggested, I consider it briefly, but it is usually promptly rejected.

However, when a second person suggests the same idea, it deserves greater consideration. Even though the risks are still there, and the rewards are still unknown, I usually give it a little more consideration. Still, I ultimately dismiss it.

A third suggestion, though, changes the game. Three people telling me the same thing is my tipping point. Instead of thinking of reasons why the idea *won't* work, I change my perspective and ask myself, *"How can I make this work?"* It is enlightening to look at things from a totally different perspective, exploring the possibilities rather than the pitfalls. After doing this, I can usually develop a strategy for trying the idea.

Therefore, in these cases, I implement a "Rule of Three": If three people tell me the same thing, then I will assume there is merit in the idea. And often, THE CREATOR speaks to us directly through other people. Especially when we are too busy, stubborn, distracted, fearful, or in denial of the truth right in front of our face.

IT ALSO WORKS IN REVERSE

Unfortunately, this "Rule of Three" works in reverse. If one person criticizes you for something, we quickly dismiss it by thinking: *He's stupid, he's biased, he's jealous, he doesn't like me, etc.* But when a third person says, "Bill, you're really being selfish here," those people probably have a point, even if they are your enemies, and you may need to work on that personal deficiency.

Bottom line: If you hear the same criticism repeatedly, there is a problem with *you*, not the people criticizing. However, that does give you an opportunity for self-improvement.

LISTEN, THEN ACT

It sounds as if Shantelle has been beyond The Rule of Three for some time. This means she should put together a portfolio and send it to a modeling agency.

In your life, follow this Rule of Three. If three people tell you the same thing, they probably can see something you can't. Listen to what they are saying, then go for it!

ADDENDUM: REAL LIFE EXAMPLE (THAT YOU ARE CURRENTLY HOLDING IN YOUR HANDS!).

In the foreword of this book, I explained the purpose behind *Deep Heavy Stuff.* I wrote about complex subjects to help whoever read it, even if it was just one person. Even though I had already written two books and was finishing up the third, I had not intended *Deep Heavy Stuff* to become a book.

My friend Estella was the first to suggest something more.

"You're going to make *Deep Heavy Stuff* a book like your other writings, right?" she asked in an email.

I responded politely but dismissed the idea. These writings were not meant to be a book. I am a humor author first and foremost, I have three humor books, and this book would be a severe and jarring left turn. I already know what I want for my fourth book. I don't have the time for this project. And so on.

Unfortunately, I don't remember the second person who suggested this. I do know that I made a mental note that I was at #2 in the Rule of Three. But I still was not going ahead with the project.

I reached #3 in September 2021 at an author fair held outdoors (due to the pandemic). I was close to wrapping up when my good friend Chris walked behind the picnic table where I was set up. She sat down beside me on the bench, looked me square in the eye, and said, "You know you must do a *Deep Heavy Stuff* book, don't you?"

Chris is an intelligent and feisty woman. This was more than a suggestion—this felt like a direct order.

I stammered a bit and said I was considering it (Sort of a lie). Chris meets the definition of a good friend by far!

But at that point, either I put together the book, or I am a hypocrite who blatantly doesn't follow his own advice. So I do hope you are benefiting from this book so far. And you can thank Chris for it.

BE THERE

This isn't going where you think it is ...

Many years ago, I worked with Debra, a beautiful, vivacious blonde. She was intelligent, pleasant, funny, and what men would describe as "sexy". We became good friends soon after she was hired. When she was promoted, our friendship became even stronger, as I became her boss.

She shared everything about her life with me, including the struggles of being a divorced mother raising her daughter. There were frequent personal conversations in my office, some with the door closed but visible to everyone through the glass wall.

And in the office, there were plenty of rumors about the nature of our relationship. When a coworker inquired about our private discussions, Debra replied, "You have husbands and boyfriends to discuss stuff with; I have Don Ake."

However, there was nothing illicit in the relationship. Even with a strong emotional and even a physical attraction between us, there were walls. This was the best job Debra ever had, so she would not jeopardize it by banging her boss. And I was happily married with two young daughters. I was not going to risk that, not even for a hot, sexy blonde.

My close relationship with Debra ended when I left the company. I had already turned in my notice when a coworker couldn't resist making one more inquiry, partially in jest, about whether Debra and I were romantically involved.

Debra responded, "No, we've never done anything. But he's not my boss anymore, is he?"

I got the impression that she may not have been joking.

Even though she was a close friend, I was hesitant to stay in touch. Now that her "wall" was gone, I wasn't sure I could resist the temptation if she wanted to be more than friends.

I had no contact with her for over two years. But then, I lost my job and had reached out to her as part of networking in my job search.

But when I called her at work, I got the horrible news that Debra had committed suicide ten days earlier.

Debra's life had completely fallen apart. Her ex-husband had finally succeeded in taking their daughter away from her. Debra had been in a serious relationship with a guy who physically abused her. And the result of all these actions was that a beautiful, extraordinary woman was dead.

My sorrow was deep and excruciating. Then came the flood of guilt:

If only I had called a couple of months ago, maybe I could have saved her.

I just missed … I just missed the funeral.

Who knows what would have happened if I had called earlier? And maybe I was fortunate not to have seen the casket; it would have burned in my memory forever.

But I am sure that if I hadn't left the company, Debra would probably be alive today. I was her close friend. I would have known the anguish these horrible events had given her. I would have defended her, supported her, and helped her.

I would have BEEN THERE.

And that's when the guilt ended, and the anger set in. Because even though I wasn't there, somebody else needed to Be There for her. Debra needed someone—anyone—to Be There, and no one was. No one. And because no one was there, a terrible tragedy occurred.

And don't tell me I shouldn't feel guilty because I no longer do. Due to the circumstances, this was not my responsibility, but someone needed to see the situation and act. And this message is not about me—it's about us. It's about you.

We have a responsibility to our friends. THE BOOK asks the question, "Am I my brother's keeper?" within the first few pages. It is not a rhetorical one. As we read through to the last page, we learn that the answer is, "Yes, we are our brother's keeper", with instruction and guidance on how to do it.

Because sometimes your friends don't need "someone", they need YOU. They need YOUR wisdom, guidance, life experience, compassion, support, and maybe just your presence. Sometimes, all a person needs to know is that someone—anyone—freakin' cares about them and what they are going through.

Be that person. Be There.

And yes, this will often be inconvenient, time-consuming, uncomfortable, and awkward. We will struggle with what to say, what to do, how to help, how to respond. You don't have to have all the answers. But maybe you know people who can help.

Your presence is much more powerful than you think. No one should have to face their problems, struggles, and demons alone.

Show up. Be There.

I never want to cry beside a friend's casket who needed my help but never got it. We need to Be There.

So Be There. Please Be There. When someone needs you to Be There for them, Be There. Just Be There.

Be There.

This Is Not the End

Author's Note: And the final essay in this chapter is me being a friend to you. Or a friend to your friend who needs to hear this message. So let me be there as a friend even though we've never met. Please feel free to reproduce the following essay and send it to someone in need.

This is not the end ...

This is not even close to the end ...

I understand it feels like the end

You think that it's the end

But **this is not the end ...**

Imagine I am sitting across from you right now

Open your eyes wide and look at me

Reach over and grab my hand

Take a deep breath

Focus on every word that follows because this is so important to you and to me

Even though your mind is spinning, relax for a moment, and just focus on my words

Take another deep breath ...

Exhale ...

Relax ...

I can tell you are in the dark place

I have been to the dark place myself

It's the worst place to be, but it won't get any worse tomorrow

Yes, tomorrow—because this is not the end

Don't believe that you will feel this bad forever—you won't.

This is the worst of it, and it can and will get better soon

Just focus on getting to tomorrow

This is not the end ...

In the dark place, you can't trust your feelings because they are spinning out of control

But eventually, the turmoil will stop, and peace will return

You also can't trust your thinking because your emotions are messing up your mind

So I'm asking you to trust me and trust every word I say

I swear what I'm telling you is accurate, based on a long life of ups and downs and one trip to the dark place you find yourself in right now

Take another deep breath ....

Exhale...

Yes, you are angry, and you have every right to be

People can be mean, stupid, vengeful, and uncaring

They have hurt you badly, and you are so mad at them

But the anger now has been turned inward on yourself

However, the problem is with them, not you

These people will still be awful tomorrow and the day after that

You can't change that, but don't let the awful people make you hate yourself

 Do not give them that power over you

Let the anger inside you flow outward

Slam your fist on the table! Scream if you need to!

Just as you need to exhale, release some of the pressure that's been building inside you

This is not the end ...

This is about you, your life, your well-being

Not them

So let's focus on you

You may feel hopeless—you may even think you are hopeless

That's how you ended up in the dark place—that's how I got there

But you do have hope—you are not hopeless—there is always hope available if you want to grasp it

There are people, good people, who will help you get your hope back

This is not the end ...

In the darkness, all you see is darkness

But your world has not come crashing down

It's still there

You just can't see it in the darkness

Your life has value, which you will see once you get out of the dark place

There is a future, and it's not far away

But in the darkness, there is no light

Once the light is turned on, you can see things as they are—not just the darkness

Just turn on the light—look at the world around you, not the things in the bad place

Focus on what is going on in the outside, not the pain on the inside

Look beyond this moment, and then start to move forward to get out of the dark place

Get to a place outside the darkness

This is not the end ...

Now, I will ask you to start to move past the dark place and into the light

I want you to ask God to help you leave the darkness

It doesn't matter if you have never prayed before

It doesn't matter if it's been a long time since you prayed

It doesn't even matter if you doubt that God exists

And most importantly, it doesn't matter if you've prayed in the past but have given up on God

Reach out to God right now, tell Him how badly you hurt

Tell Him how angry you are. Cry out and ask Him to help you

And I assure you, with every fiber of my being, that you will receive help

That you will feel cared for, and that you will start moving out of the dark place

Pray now, then resume reading this

And now, find someone to talk to about what you are going through and how you feel

Call your best friend, or call the kindest, most caring person you know

Tell them you urgently need to talk to them

And once again, they will listen

Trust me on this

Yes, some bad people hurt you, but there are good people who will help you. You just need to ask

In the darkness, you can't see us, but we are here

We are everywhere—just ask—just please ask

If you don't want to talk to someone you know, call the largest church near you, and tell them you need to talk to a pastor right now

They will listen, and they will help you

If you have no one you feel comfortable talking to, then please call 800-273-8255

This is not the end ...

Tomorrow may not be a good day, but it will be a better day

Please trust me on this. **This is not the end**

PART II
DEALING WITH HARDSHIP & OTHER LIFE CHALLENGES

CHAPTER 7:
OVERCOMING REJECTION, FAILURE, AND TRAGEDY

Life is a series of ups and downs. No one can escape the bad times. However, how we respond to loss, failure, and tragedy varies significantly among individuals. Two people can suffer the same fate, but one endures without much turmoil, while the other is damaged for life, the event even having possibly triggered a mental illness. This chapter is not about just dealing with tragedy, but it's specifically for those who let their emotions spin out of control, enter a downward spiral, and hit rock bottom. Hitting the bottom is deep, heavy stuff.

Many people have hit bottom at some point in their life. Some made poor decisions, while others suffered a tragedy entirely out of their control. Either way, your wealth, status, age, race, faith, etc. doesn't matter because how we react to hitting the bottom is based on how our brain and emotions function. It's therefore a combination of genetics and experience, two things we don't have much control over.

From the outside, it's easy to judge someone and wonder why they are taking the unfortunate event so hard. However, you can't see what's going on inside their mind. You don't know their thoughts or the turmoil they are going through. You think, *"It's not that bad. They'll recover in no time."* However, that's not true. If they really have hit bottom, it will be a long trip back.

If you have ever hit bottom, this chapter will remind you how far you've come and how important it is to help others who are currently at the bottom. If you are at the bottom and struggling to recover—which can take months if not years—let this chapter encourage you to persevere. Let every word sink in. Believe what I'm saying is trustworthy and reread certain portions every day. If you are one of the fortunate ones who have never experienced "hitting bottom", take this opportunity to gain an understanding of what people around you may be going through. Show empathy and help them. When someone is recovering from a tragedy, it is human nature to abandon them. However, if you get only one thing from this chapter, it's that your friends sometimes desperately need you. Be there for them.

When You Hit Bottom

Life is going along fine, maybe even wonderfully, when an unexpected tragedy knocks you off your perch. You fall, and you keep falling. Your head spins as the life you knew slips through your fingers. The turmoil is intense. You try to grab on to something, anything that will stop the fall, but there's only air. You experience a torrent of destructive emotions all hitting you at once. You are so overwhelmed—you can't think, you can't cry, you can hardly breathe. It's just one long, loud, internal scream.

And then comes the abrupt crash at the end. Of course, you don't hear a thud, but the force of the blow still shakes your inner core. It hammers your soul. It's quietly painful and painfully quiet at the same time.

You have hit bottom.

If you have never experienced this feeling, please keep reading. You need to understand what happens when a friend or family member hits bottom. It will help you say the right things and do the right things. Believe it or not, how you act could make the difference between your friend recovering and staying in that dark place for years to come.

If you have previously hit bottom, this chapter will remind you just how far you've come.

And if you're at the bottom right now, read this slowly and understand that I know how it feels, and my words are true, to the best of my ability to express them. Though we may have never met and will likely never see each other in person, I will do my best to grab you and pull you out.

Many times, it is difficult to understand why someone has hit bottom. People looking at my situation from the outside would have said, *"He has a great life. He'll bounce back. This is just a temporary setback. He has nothing to worry about."*

But our brains are complex organs. Once you start to fall, you do not think logically. Once your emotions spin out of control, you cannot stop the downward spiral. While things may seem fine on the outside looking in, the situation on the inside is a horrible mess.

Some people reading this will not understand how it feels to have your emotions spin out of control during awful circumstances. If this is you, then great. Because I wouldn't want my worst enemy to experience this.

But if your mood swings from highest highs to lowest lows, it is difficult to stabilize yourself after you've fallen so far. And it doesn't matter what your status is: rich, poor, educated, uneducated... The bottom doesn't discriminate.

And regardless of the circumstances, all "bottom-dwellers" will find some reason to blame themselves for their predicament: Even when it's not your fault, at the bottom, you will savagely beat yourself up because somehow, it IS your fault.

And this tendency to judge people because they deserved it? In THE BOOK, when THE MAN encounters someone at the bottom, He is not concerned about how they got there. Instead, He is totally focused on helping them renew their life.

We tend to make excuses for not helping these people based on whether we feel they deserved their fate or how bad their situation is to us. This is the wrong approach. The person at the bottom desperately needs to know that someone cares. They feel alone, forsaken, abandoned. Just telling someone that you care about them or lending them a hand means more than you can ever imagine.

THREE BENEFITS

Now, there are actually three benefits to hitting the bottom:

1. You can't fall any farther. That plunge was traumatic and frightening, but you are on solid ground now. It may be a low point, but it is the endpoint. You can't go lower than this.
2. There is no confusion about which direction to go. There are no choices. There are no options. There is only one way out: straight up. Once you focus, you can move in one direction with no detours.

3. It's eerily quiet at the bottom. There are few distractions. If you want to hear the voice of THE CREATOR, just listen. He has your attention, so take advantage of this situation to gather wisdom, hope, and resolve.

HOW IT FEELS

When you hit bottom, figuratively, you land face-first. This means initially, you lie there staring at the ground. You are focused on the ground and how you ended up there. You focus on the past. You are obsessed with the specific details that brought you here. You rewind the Hell over and over in your mind, and the pain and the burden are immense. It's like playing the same horror movie repeatedly, and you are always the star of the show.

Therefore, step one in recovery is rolling over and staring at the sky. That represents your future. Up: That's where you are headed. But it's still a struggle because you continue to think irrationally, but you don't realize it. Your mind is confused because your emotions are overwhelming it. You can't trust your thoughts at the bottom because you'll be telling yourself lies like these:

- *There is no way out of this mess.*
- *It's always going to be this bad.*
- *I'm always going to feel this torment.*
- *My useful, relevant life has ended.*
- *I am a loser, and I will always be a loser.*

And a host of other negative thoughts based on your situation and background.

Understand that these are complete, utter lies. For emphasis: THESE ARE TOTAL LIES. They seem trustworthy at the time because they are coming from inside your head, but under stress, you will deceive yourself. You will tell yourself these lies repeatedly until you believe they are true. But trust me, all lies. All false. Be honest enough to tell a friend or counselor what you're telling yourself, and they will also tell you that these thoughts are all lies.

Those of us who have climbed out know that these thoughts are lies. They seem ludicrous now: "*My useful, relevant life has ended?*" Oh, I believed that one when I lost my job of 16 years. But after writing three books, being repeatedly quoted in the Wall Street Journal, and having people fly me around the country to hear me speak? That one was the biggest lie ever.

But from the pit, you can't see your future. You can only see your failure—or your current, dire circumstances. It's challenging to look forward even a year into the future when you are obsessed with just making it through the day. But there will be a future, and, as in my case, that future may be greater than you could ever imagine. It will be much different than your past, but it will be your future, a future that you have the power and ability to build, so embrace it and create it.

Dwelling on your past mistakes or misfortunes while trying to recover is like driving a car forward by looking through the rear-view mirror. You can't go very fast or very straight, and you may not even go very far. So you must rip that mirror off the car. There is no need for it since there's only one direction: forward.

IT'S WHAT YOU STILL HAVE

I moved slowly and deliberately across the room to greet her. As I approached, I noticed her hollow eyes. It was as if all the life had been totally sucked out of her—and in a way, it had. She appeared frail and transparent; I could practically see right through her. She couldn't hide her pain, so she didn't try. I could feel her overwhelming agony. She radiated anguish.

She had lost her husband of over twenty years. It was sudden and unexpected. Her plunge to the bottom was deep and rapid, and the crash was severe. This was by no fault of her own, and yet she probably found a way to blame herself because that's the type of irrational thinking you experience at the bottom.

It was the first time I had seen Cindy since the funeral seven months ago. I hoped she would have been doing better by now. But how could I know what to expect, never having experienced a loss this devastating?

Her condition caught me off guard. I would speak to her in a few seconds, but what could I possibly say? I couldn't ask, "How's it going?" because she was going through hell, and I didn't want her to have to describe the trip. In fact, all small talk was out because it's small, and what we had here was trauma. Enormous trauma.

My brain started spinning, trying to find the right words to say. I'm a positive person, and I don't function well in negative situations, so my rule is to let my words be few. So, after the customary hellos, I blurted out:

"It's going to get better."

Cindy's expression reflects a complete rejection of my statement.

"It's going to get better," I repeat.

This time, she scrunches her face and turns her head. She is hurting so badly, and the idea is so inconceivable she can't even verbally express her feelings. She can't even imagine a future because the present hurts so badly.

"Trust me. It's going to get better." Repeated for yet a third time in a softer, reassuring tone.

How did I know it was going to get better? What I saw in front of me was a beautiful, smart, charming woman. A woman with terrific children and an incredible family supporting her, half of her life still yet to be lived.

But Cindy couldn't see that.

You plummet to the bottom because you lost something: a person, a spouse, a relationship, a job, a status, an income, an asset, your dignity, your health, and so on. And at the bottom, all you can see is what you lost, not *what you still have.* We agonize over the loss. We obsess over the loss. We want the lost thing back so desperately. We yearn to go back in time. But that can't happen.

What you still have after the fall is so vitally important. It's what you will build upon as you move forward. It is the platform on which your recovery begins. It is your base; it is your core. And that doesn't disappear, no matter how far you have fallen.

So, to repeat with emphasis:

**IT'S NOT WHAT YOU LOST THAT'S IMPORTANT—
IT'S WHAT YOU STILL HAVE.**

Several months after that, I could tell Cindy was coping better, but the grieving process continued. My message to her was the same:

"It's going to get better."

"I hope so," she replied.

When I saw the hope in her eyes, I knew she was on her way back. She was climbing out. She was gaining the strength to move forward.

But she had still lost something precious: a great husband and a great man. Her life had been rich, richer than she'd ever realized until it had been so suddenly shaken. Cindy's recovery was going to take some time.

And then it happened: Her life improved. Then, her life became good. And then, her life became great once again. I don't know if her life now is better than it was before the tragedy, but it might be just as good. Regardless, Cindy was able to build on the qualities she already had and learn to live again. She thought her life was over, but it was far from finished because:

It's not what you lost that's ultimately important. It's what you still have.

THE LONG CLIMB OUT

It only takes a second to fall—from your pedestal, your position, your place, or your life—into the pit. The unexpected meeting, phone call, text message, tragedy, diagnosis, overdose, etc. changes your life in an instant. The cruel reality is that even though the plunge is sudden, the climb out is long and arduous.

One must scratch and claw their way out of the pit, learning to celebrate small victories against sturdy resistance. The maximum weights have been placed on the barbell, and now you must become strong enough to lift it.

And you will. Through the process, you will gain the strength, the guts, the determination, the grit, and the skills to flourish in your next challenge in life. You pray, and you work, and you pray some more.

The process of climbing out of your despair is grueling. For many people, it's the most difficult challenge they will ever face. It is painfully slow and full of repeated setbacks. Your lack of visible progress will be frustrating, but you must move forward at your own pace, just keep moving forward. You may have to crawl, but just like an infant, you must learn to crawl before you walk. And to walk before you run.

And you will fail and fail repeatedly. And you will lose and lose repeatedly. You will lose so often that people will consider you a loser. At times, you will feel like a loser. But let me assure you: If you are still in the game; if you are still at the table; if when you breathe in, your lungs receive oxygen, you are not a loser. You are a warrior who has not yet achieved the victory. Resilience is the most valuable trait you can possess. Crawl on, walk on, run on—move forward.

Until you finally break out. It may take years, but the effort is worth it. You can emerge stronger, better, and more resilient for your efforts.

Life at the bottom is brutal, but it can be empowering if you let it.

RESILIENCE, PERSISTENCE, PERSEVERANCE

Through my life experience, including my climb out of the pit, I believe that one of the most valuable traits you can possess is resilience.

Oxford Languages defines *"resilience"* as:

1. *the capacity to recover quickly from difficulties; toughness.*
2. *the ability of a substance or object to spring back into shape; elasticity.*

If you have resilience, you can endure almost anything life throws at you and bounce back. If you still have air in your lungs and the diagnosis is not terminal, then you will come fighting back.

However, saying you want to be "resilient" is like saying you want to climb Mt. Everest. You may achieve your goal, but not without extensive training, effort, and much pain. In order to become resilient, you must fail repeatedly.

The most valuable skill you acquire during this time is the ability to recover from a failure or loss. Before your fall, a setback in your life may have plunged you into a deep despair for more than a month. But now, you will fail repeatedly. You will fail so much that at some point, it barely phases you at all. You will learn to take a punch and not be afraid to get hit again. You will learn how to get knocked down and instinctively bounce back up. You will become a human Weeble: You will wobble, but you won't fall down.

There are two other traits you will pick up along the way:

Persistence: firm or obstinate continuance in a course of action despite difficulty or opposition.

And...

Perseverance: persistence in doing something despite difficulty or delay in achieving success.

(As defined by Oxford Languages)

This is going to be a long, arduous journey, where you face difficulties and opposition. It will involve frequent losses and a long delay in getting to where you need to be.

How does perseverance work?

You tell yourself you are going to quit...

BUT YOU DO NOT QUIT!

You convince yourself that it would be better if you quit...

BUT YOU DO NOT QUIT!

You list all the advantages of quitting...

BUT YOU DO NOT QUIT!

You tell yourself you are never going to win...

BUT YOU DO NOT QUIT!

You endure emotional pain that grinds on you...

BUT YOU DO NOT QUIT!

And the grind will be heavy. You are going to lose, then lose again, and then lose some more. Lose, lose, lose, lose again.

Learning how to lose. Acquiring the skill of regaining your balance after getting knocked down. Believing in yourself. How well you do these things makes the difference of whether you stay down or bounce back up and propel forward.

You get punched in the face so often that you become impervious to the pain (This is not entirely a good thing: Pain exists for a reason). Some friends asked why I was so persistent in trying to regain my life, and the honest answer was, "Because failing didn't hurt anymore."

However, this is what it takes to ultimately achieve success. If you are committed to climbing out of the pit and getting back to where you were, this is the price you must pay. Unfortunately, the longer the fall, the longer the climb back. There are no shortcuts. You may not be responsible for ending up in the pit, but you are responsible for climbing out. So climb, and don't stop climbing.

THE PROMISE

At some point, you will face an acid test. After you have suffered failures... after people view you as a failure... when people would rather pity you than help you... your success at climbing out of the pit comes down to this:

EITHER YOU BELIEVE IN YOURSELF, OR YOU DON'T!

This is where you reach down deep and decide who you are, what you have to offer, and where you want to go. And then, you make the choice:

EITHER YOU BELIEVE IN YOURSELF, OR YOU DON'T!

It doesn't matter who else believes in you, who else cares for you, or who makes the effort to help you ...

EITHER YOU BELIEVE IN YOURSELF, OR YOU DON'T!

There will be those dark days when you feel alone and completely abandoned. You will doubt yourself. You will feel as if no one cares.

It is at those times that the people of FAITH should trust in the promise of THE CREATOR, that He will never leave you nor forsake you. And why are those words there? Why are they even in THE BOOK, when that truth seems so obvious? Precisely for these dark days. Yes, you know it's true, but you need to hear it repeatedly in your journey upward. This truth is so essential that it appears near the beginning of THE BOOK and is repeated again near the end*:

THE CREATOR will never leave you nor forsake you.

Even when everyone else has, THE CREATOR promises He won't, and that promise is all you need.

Resilience … Persistence … Perseverance.

MY STORY

Of course, the only way I could describe all of this in so much detail is to have experienced it myself. My ability as a writer is based on my capacity to feel emotions intensely and express those emotions in words.

I was plunged into the pit years ago due to the loss of a long-time job. Looking back, I should not have reacted this poorly to that event. That was a personal failure. I should not have wrapped my entire identity up in my job—or lack thereof—but I did. How I reacted was my responsibility, and it was also my responsibility to climb out of this pit.

If you charted my progress at that time, it was slow and painful. It looked like this:

Loss, loss, loss, big loss, loss, terrible loss, loss, stupid loss, loss, painful loss, dispiriting loss ……

But through this process, I learned resilience. Like a shortstop dives for a grounder and then bounces up to make the throw, I learned to rebound instinctively. It is the most valuable skill I acquired during this process.

Persistence? Oh, there was a continuous effort despite all the difficulties, all right. I was turned down by the same company five times for five different positions.

Perseverance? There was much difficulty and pain, and my climb back took several years.

After four years of battles, if my internal condition was visualized, my clothes were in tatters and featured a couple of bullet holes. My face was bruised and battered, and there were numerous bloodstains.

I had fought as hard as I could, and I had lost every battle—every single one. At that point, you could have considered me a loser. You could have pitied me.

But I never pitied myself. That just keeps you from moving forward.

And then suddenly, unexpectedly, I won the war.

I'M DONE

I had just failed to land a job at the same company for the fifth time. Obviously, I wanted to work for this company very badly, or I wouldn't have kept coming back. I was an excellent fit for the job and was probably the leading candidate, but the company had decided to eliminate the position altogether.

But this failure didn't faze me. It only hurt for a moment because I had learned to bounce right back up. In effect, I had become immune to the enduring pain this once would have caused.

That evening, I took off for my two-mile powerwalk feeling fine. But I must have been thinking about this most recent failure, as something was different this time. Typically, after a loss, I would quickly move on to the next opportunity, plan, strategy, etc. And I would have the energy and the will to pursue it.

But now, there was no next opportunity, and my desire to keep fighting was gone. Near the halfway point of my walk, I came to a distressing realization:

This challenge was coming to an end, and I had lost. I had tried as hard as I could, but it wasn't enough. It wasn't as if I was quitting—the *game clock* had hit triple-zero, and the powers that be had declared this contest was over.

I uttered a two-word prayer: *I'm done.*

It didn't mean I was done with life—more like life was done with me. And I wasn't done with THE CREATOR. It was just an admission that I could not continue this climb. I had given all I had. I was done.

The walk back home was brutal. I thought about what this downfall would mean. I was working in a job that utilized none of my skills and was failing tremendously at it. I hated the job, and the company had run out of patience with me. They had tried to get me to quit for the last four months, but I had hung on—by just a thread. Now, I was loosening my grip. I wouldn't last there much longer.

I thought about what the next few years would be like, having lost this fight. I wasn't afraid of hitting bottom again—I had been there once and survived—but I was scared I wouldn't have the strength to crawl back out again.

But prayers are one of the great mysteries of life. We think our prayers must be lengthy, eloquent pleas, filled with all sorts of bargaining and reasons why we should receive the desired result. We try to manipulate THE CREATOR by our prayers, which is an absurd concept. We do this repeatedly, and it never works out. However, we see instances in THE BOOK where people are so distraught they can't even speak the words, yet their prayers are still answered.** I have come to believe that honesty is a crucial component of prayer that we conveniently ignore. Above all else, THE CREATOR wants us to be honest.

"I'm done" on the surface seems like such a feeble prayer. It lacks fervency. It lacks substance. It even lacks faith. It is an admission of failure. It is a surrender. It is devoid of hope. Heck, I didn't even ask for anything. The only redeeming quality of this prayer is it was honest—brutally honest. "I'm done" seems so ineffectual, and yet it turned out to be the second most powerful prayer I have ever uttered.

Those two words reflected four years of striving, four years of suffering, four hard years of personal and spiritual growth. I was a much different person than I was when this challenge began, but now I sensed this struggle was coming to an end.

My instincts were indeed correct: I *was* done. This ordeal was about to come to an end, but not at all how I expected. Three weeks later, I received an email from a former colleague who said he wanted to discuss an opportunity. I didn't think this "opportunity" held much substance at all—I thought it was just a project we had previously discussed.

However...

"We have a position becoming available in a few months. We've discussed it, and we think no one can do this job better than you."

This, after not being in that industry for years. No resume. No interview. Just boom! A great job that was meant for me. A better job at a better company than I had before. And after that resurgence came the quotes in prestigious publications, speaking engagements at resorts, and the writing and publishing of three books— this one being the fourth.

Now, you could think I got lucky, but I firmly believe that most times, "you make your own luck". I had crawled out of the pit. I had stayed active. I had stayed visible. I had fought so hard. I had made progress.

So often, we become frustrated at our lack of visible progress. We dismiss each rock we climb because our eyes are on the top of the mountain. But NEVER, NEVER, disregard the progress that you have made. It is valuable ground you have secured. And often, that middle ground provides you with a launching pad to even greater things.

I had lost every battle in this conflict. I had been defeated every time. By definition, I was a loser, but I never saw myself as one. I didn't define myself that way. I pushed on, regardless of all the failures.

And in the end, I lost every battle, yet still won the war.

QUESTIONS ASKED FROM THE BOTTOM OF THAT PIT

WHY ME?

After you suffer some unexpected tragedy, it is natural to ask the question "Why Me?" I had to ponder that thought long and hard after learning my daughter had suffered brain damage at birth. This was a random occurrence. I had done nothing to deserve this. She has surely done nothing to deserve this. So: Why Me? Why did this awful thing have to happen to me?

After agonizing over this question many times, I was never able to come up with an answer. But I was also not able to answer the question: Why *not* me? The universe is random and imperfect. Tragedies occur around the world every moment. Although I had done nothing to deserve this, I also had done nothing worthy not to deserve this.

Asking "Why *not* me?" puts it in a new perspective. Why not someone else? Do I want someone else to deal with this? No, I would not have wished my predicament on my worst enemy. So, you must own your situation. This is my challenge, and I must deal with it the best I can.

Holding on to this "Why Me?" question is harmful. You never are going to answer it, and even if you could, it doesn't matter. If you dwell on this, you will view yourself as a victim, which leads to self-pity. This spirit of defeatism drags you down and holds you back from moving forward. It makes it harder to climb out of the pit.

WHY IS GOD PUNISHING ME?

I believe everyone has asked themselves this question at one time. Even though theologians have debated this question for eons, let me give you the simple answer: "God is not punishing you."

If God were to punish you right now for every sin and indiscretion you have ever committed, you would instantly be reduced to a pile of ashes, blown away like dust in the wind. So, God didn't punish you by putting you in the hospital or unemployment line.

God did not punish you. Most likely, you suffered a random fate brought forth from an imperfect universe. However, this same universe is capable of punishment if you risk fate. If you engage in risky behavior, fast driving, substance abuse, etc., God didn't punish you, you did that to yourself.

Even if you truly believe God punished you for some sin, and I can't really say that *never* happens, He provides a way out. It's called repentance. Besides the spiritual aspects of this act, the practical benefit is that it allows us to move forward, and not be stuck in the past. And repentance is not limited to God. You may also apologize to those you have wronged (like in *A Christmas Carol*) as a way of starting over.

WHERE DID ALL MY FRIENDS GO?

A cruel reality of life is people like to associate with winners and avoid losers. You ended up in the pit because you lost something important. Therefore, you are considered a loser by many. Many people you considered friends will abandon you. These were never real friends, but just associates. In the pit, you will find out who your real friends are. Good friends will stand by you. Great friends will help pull you out of the pit.

Remember forever those people who didn't abandon you. Help them as much as you can because they are true friends, and you owe them a huge debt of gratitude for being there when you needed them. And help pull your friends out of that pit when they fall or fail. Because you know how it feels and you know how important a true friend can be in this situation.

'* Deuteronomy 31:6 and Hebrews 13:5

'** 1 Samuel 1:12-16

CHAPTER 8:
ON DEATH AND GRIEVING

Death is the deepest, heaviest stuff there is. This chapter includes stories about the deaths of friends and how I struggled in the aftermath. I hope that by sharing these personal feelings, it helps you understand your own responses and enables you to grieve and cope better.

Also in this chapter, there is practical advice on how to help others who are in the grieving process. Many of us could improve our approach in this area. Finally, there is an essay on the pain we feel when our dog dies.

GRAHAM IS GONE ...

Graham was one of the first friends I'd made at The University of Akron, and he was my best friend from my college days—excluding my wife, of course.

I can't remember how we met. I do know, however, that we hit it off immediately. We were two intelligent guys from blue-collar roots. We both had a great sense of humor, loved to laugh, and didn't take the world too seriously. But now it is serious—deadly serious—because...

Graham is gone—and he left this place much too soon.

We also shared a love for contemporary Christian music, which had just started gaining popularity at the time. Over the years, we talked about how organized churches were doing it all wrong. We even imagined starting our own church and doing it right, even though we weren't pastors. But that will never happen now because...

Graham is gone—and he left this place much too soon.

Graham and I thought it was amusing that we were good friends despite our high schools being fierce rivals. In later years, to the delight of many, we would pretend to have these high school-inspired fights on Facebook. But the rivalry has ended because...

Graham is gone—and he left this place much too soon.

Graham was the most intelligent person I ever knew. He had a doctorate and worked for a time at NASA. Yes, he was a rocket scientist. But you would never know it. He never imposed his intellect on anyone. You would think he was just an average guy with average smarts. Graham and I would have these deep discussions where we would try to solve the world's problems, even though we knew no one would ever listen to hooligans like us. But those discussions are over because...

Graham is gone—and he left this place much too soon.

After college, Graham attended my wedding, and I would occasionally run into him at concerts. But like most people, we lost touch. He left his job at NASA in Cleveland and worked at an aeronautics firm in New Jersey instead.

However, we were able to reconnect by the wonder that is Facebook. I can't remember who friended who, but the relationship was renewed. But it was about this time that his life began to change. His marriage ended at about the same time as his New Jersey job. He moved back to Ohio, which meant we could occasionally meet. But there will be no more meetings because...

Graham is gone—and he left this place much too soon.

Graham was fed up with the corporate establishment, so he now worked jobs way below his skill level. He and a partner formed a nonprofit designed to reduce bullying in schools. I even invested in the organization myself to support my friend.

He also fell in love with a lovely Filipina woman who he met on Facebook. No matter how you may view this relationship, he loved her—of that, I am sure. Right, wrong, crazy, stupid—I don't care. He genuinely loved her. And that was good enough for me. I also believe she truly loved him. Based on my correspondence with her, she is a good person. She is not a fake.

They wanted to marry and went through the expensive and arduous government requirements to make that happen. I even wrote a recommendation letter as part of the process. Once the final paperwork was approved, Graham's fiancée would fly here, and they would wed.

Graham needed money for her plane ticket and final government fees, so he started a GoFundMe campaign. Surely, with all his Facebook friends, he could quickly raise all the necessary funds and more, right? However, he didn't receive many contributions. What he did get were many derisive posts critical of his actions. The comments hurt him, but they didn't diminish his love for the woman one bit.

The lesson here: Don't publicly criticize the personal decisions of others when it is none of your d@mn business. It serves no purpose but to hurt the person, and it makes you look whiny and hateful.

I supported my friend because he is my friend, and I knew how important this was to him. But only three people donated money to his campaign—only three. He collected $535. The other two donors gave $20 and $15, respectively.

You can do the math.

But tragically, the visa application was denied at the last moment by the Philippine government. Graham was crushed and his fiancée heartbroken. I never got my money back, but that was okay with me. Graham tried to pay me back by helping to promote my books, but he owes me no longer because...

Graham is gone—and he left this place much too soon.

Then, Graham suffered a severe stroke. One of those that you almost wish you didn't survive. He went through extensive physical therapy and made remarkable progress. He looked healthy and seemed to be committed to surviving this trauma.

But the stroke and the broken engagement changed Graham, and not for the better. He became bitter and more argumentative. He became much more serious. I didn't like the "new" Graham, but now, looking back, how could he not be bitter? His life had been greatly diminished by little if any fault of his own.

The lesson here: Our long-time friends can change due to physical and mental issues we don't see. We need to cut them some slack.

Graham even argued with me, and not like those pleasant debates of our college days. But there will be no more arguments, pleasant or otherwise, because...

Graham is gone—and he left this place much too soon.

The next time I had lunch with Graham, it was apparent he was not taking care of himself like he had after the stroke. I think he had figured out that he didn't have much time left, so he may as well get as much out of life as he could. He hadn't given up on life—life had given up on him. But there will be no more lunches because ...

Graham is gone—and he left this place much too soon.

His condition deteriorated. He moved to Pennsylvania to stay with his son. He hated to be a burden, but he had no choice.

On his last visit to Ohio, we were supposed to get together. He texted me late on his visit. But I told him I was engrossed in watching a football game and that "I would catch him next time". But there will be no next time because ....

Graham is gone—and he left this place much too soon.

A few months ago, I got an early morning message from his former fiancée. She'd heard Graham had passed and wanted me to confirm. He had posted earlier that week that he was really sick and maybe it was COVID, but not to worry. However, his Facebook posts indicated his health had been deteriorating for months. I sadly had to message back to the woman...

Graham is gone—and he left this place much too soon.

And now, as I pass through middle age, these sad texts and messages become much too frequent. I can better deal with what aging is doing to my body than what it is doing to my old friends. And this one hurt, but it must be endured, because there will be more. But for now...

Graham is gone—and he left this place much too soon.

THE SORROW WAS TOO STRONG

Tim Richardson was the best person I have ever known. At my age, I doubt I will meet anyone better. He was my brother-in law, and it was terrific having such a terrific person as your brother-in-law. One of the best decisions in my life was marrying into that family. I would hear friends and colleagues complain about their terrible in-laws, then ask me what problems I had with mine.

I would reply, "None. I married into the Waltons*."

And Tim was the best of the bunch.

Tim died suddenly and tragically at age 47 due to a blood clot that traveled up to his heart. I wrote the following Facebook posts soon afterward. They appear here verbatim—as written with only minor edits—to preserve the raw emotion of that time:

THE NEWS (APRIL 2, 2013)

Today at around 3 p.m. my wife called to tell me that her youngest brother, Tim Richardson, had unexpectedly passed away. It would be difficult to know a finer person or to have a better brother-in-law. Heavy grieving.

THE PAIN

I apologize to my family for not being able to offer any comments of support or condolences at this time. I hurt, I just hurt, so incredibly bad .....

THE TRIBUTES

#1 – Tribute to my brother-in-law Tim Richardson who passed away Tuesday: Last year Tim and I served as pallbearers at his father's military funeral. There are strict rules on handling the casket and they asked for two volunteers from the pallbearers to assist with the closing of the casket. I immediately volunteered. I really did not want anything to do with closing anyone's casket, but I didn't want Tim to have to go through that with his own father. I was relieved when someone behind me

immediately raised their hand also. That was until I turned around and saw that the other volunteer was Tim. I pulled him aside and strongly protested. "You do not have to do this. You should not have to do this", I said sternly. "It's okay, I want to do this", he said calmly. That ended the argument because I was totally speechless. He wanted to do that? Who wants to do that? I don't want to do that for a stranger, let alone a parent. Yet Tim saw that as his responsibility and actually wanted to fulfill it.

#2 – A Tribute to my brother-in-law Tim Richardson who passed away April 2: In February 2012 the family was jammed into a crowded hospital waiting room because my father-in-law was critically ill. Someone walking by, spilled a cup of ice on the floor. Most of the ice fell harmlessly on the carpet, but a couple pieces fell on the tile walkway, creating a safety hazard. I was seated against the wall and the ice was behind where Tim was standing.

I pointed to the ice and told Tim to kick the cubes back onto the carpet. Instead of doing that, Tim picked up the ice on the tile and then proceeded to pick up every other piece of ice on the carpet and throw them in the trash. Once again, I was just amazed by this act. Unbelievably, one of the people in the other family made some snarky comment and seemed upset that Tim had cleaned up their mess.

Some people never seem to do what is required in life. I guess I try to get by doing only what is required. Tim was exceptional because he tried to do more than what was required, even when under stress in a hospital waiting room.

#3 – A tribute to Tim Richardson, my brother-in-law, who passed away April 2: Two years ago I adopted a new philosophy: I want to live my life in such a way that people cry at my funeral. Easy to say, hard to do. Some days I do accomplish this, most days I fail.

I never thought about what the scene might look like if a person was actually able to live a life that cherished. But now I know, because last Friday night I sat by myself in the corner of a funeral home and watched intently as the line of mourners moved past the casket. I have never been in the presence of so much sorrow ever before. And there is a difference between sorrow and sadness. Sadness is a surface emotion. Sadness is expressed because the person is deceased. Sorrow is a deep emotion and expressed because the person is no longer here. We are now missing something beloved, someone that we will never have in this realm again.

And sitting in the midst of this sorrow, I began to absorb it, to breathe it in. And the human body can only hold so much sorrow at one time, so at some point I had to escape the melancholy and retreat outside. And there at the edge of the parking lot, the sorrow absorbed in the previous 80 minutes poured out of me. This was a life well lived, very well lived, indeed.

#4 – Tribute to my friend (and brother-in-law) Tim Richardson who passed away April 2: On February 11, my wife's family met for dinner at a Fairlawn restaurant to commemorate some occasion that I can't even recall. I do remember that I wasn't really looking forward to the

event since it was on a Monday night and we would have to rush to get there and then get home late.

At the table, Tim was seated to my immediate right. Looking back, this wasn't unusual. At most family events, Tim and I usually hung out together. This wasn't by any conscious choice. I just liked being around him because he was such a great guy. He wasn't just my brother-in-law, he was my friend. And I know that type of relationship does not exist in every family. I am extremely fortunate to have married into a tremendous family and Tim was a big part of that.

I never really thought about the friendship part of the relationship. Tim was just a great brother-in-law. We never argued and I can't remember having any conflicts with him in the 35 years that I knew him.

The February dinner was great. Everyone had a good time and we laughed boisterously trying to decide what each person should order from the restaurant's extensive menu. At the end of the meal, I said goodbye to Tim as I had done hundreds of times before. Only this time it wasn't just goodbye, it turned out it was, GOODBYE. It's now time not to be so concerned about the inconvenience of rushing to get to places or getting home late.

THE REFLECTION

In December I was able to do two unexpected (and unrequired) acts of generosity for my brother-in-law Tim. At the time I considered them relatively small and insignificant. Upon his untimely passing this Tuesday, I realize that I was able to provide two blessings to him in what turned out to be the last few months of his life. Now these acts to me seem magnanimous, they are almost immeasurable. How is it that my perspective on this was so far off? What "small" acts did I have the chance to do today for other people that I did not do? What opportunities will I have tomorrow?

* a reference to the fictional family from the 1970's TV show of the same name

CANADIAN CLAUDE HAS GONE TO MEET HIS CANADIAN GOD

It was very early the first day of my vacation at Amelia Island, and I was looking forward to a time of peace, relaxation, and solitude in this Florida paradise. But on my Facebook feed, I see the heartbreaking news that my friend Claude has died unexpectedly.

I worked with Claude for several years. He was our Canadian sales rep, and it was always a pleasure to see him when he would visit the home office. I was sad when he was downsized from our company, a fate I would also experience just seven months later.

Afterwards, we kept in touch. He was the first social media contact I ever had, asking me to connect on something called "LinkedIn". We later connected on Facebook and exchanged many messages, memes, and laughs over the years. After I started working again in the same industry, I would talk to Claude at his new sales job several times a year to get his insight into the Canadian market. And just four months prior to this Florida vacation, I'd had lunch with him at a trade show.

And now, suddenly, he was gone. Some hidden health issue had taken him down. I was deeply saddened. For some reason, it hurt more because my only Canadian friend was gone. I don't travel internationally, so I don't have friends around the world. Losing Claude had shrunken my world.

I was conflicted because I was supposed to be enjoying life on the beach, but now, I was experiencing grief over losing a friend. It did not help that the night before, I'd heard that my classmate Bob had passed away as well. The vacation had just been filled with bad news so far.

The only way I could enjoy my vacation and pay respect to my friend at the same time was to create my own personal dirge. And to repeat that dirge over and over in my head anytime I thought about Claude:

Canadian Claude has gone to meet his Canadian God.

You might consider it silly, even disrespectful, but every time I thought of Claude—and it was often—over the next several days...

Canadian Claude has gone to meet his Canadian God.

Canadian Claude has gone to meet his Canadian God.

Canadian Claude has gone to meet his Canadian God.

However, it was effective. This simple lament enabled me to have a great vacation and acknowledge my grief at the same time.

When I returned home, I was able to reflect upon Claude, our friendship, and life in general. I even donated money, going through the steps to send funds internationally, to the charity designated by his family.

I was still grieving Claude's death a couple of weeks later. I thought this unusual, since although he was a good friend, he wasn't really a *close* friend. However, I think you respond to the death of someone your age in different ways depending on where you are in life. The first is when you are young, and every death is tragic and unexpected. The second is when you reach middle age, and the deaths of your peer group steadily increase. They may still "die too soon", but now, these deaths are often due to "natural causes" and therefore seem more natural. In the third stage, the deaths become expected: "He was 89 years old. He was lucky to make it that far."

I believe Claude's death—he was five years younger than me at the time—was my progression from stage one to stage two. This created psychological stress, which I struggled to deal with. Even now, some of my friends are having trouble realizing that death is edging closer.

One morning back at home, while I was brushing my teeth, I was trying to figure out why Claude's death was still bothering me so much. I asked myself who Claude had reminded me of most in my life.

Then, I looked in the mirror.

Oh, so that's it …

HER HOURGLASS RAN OUT OF SAND

Eight weeks ago, my good friend Darla* messaged me with the distressing news that she had been diagnosed with liver cancer. We had seen each other for the first time since the pandemic at my book signing event a few weeks prior.

We had made plans to have breakfast, and now, there was some urgency to schedule it. We had met at a networking event several years ago, and we would periodically have breakfast or see each other at business socials. She had gone through a terrible divorce, and I'd helped coach her through it. She was now reaching out for help through this trial.

At breakfast, I had expected a somber discussion, but Darla was just as cheery as ever, with a dazzling smile and delightful laugh. She said the prognosis was good, and she would be fine after a few weeks of chemo. They were running more tests, but she was convinced she was not in danger.

What she was telling me did not match how she was acting. I wondered if she could be in denial. There were some serious things I wanted to discuss with Darla, but she was so positive, I didn't want to quell her optimism. Maybe the real purpose of this meeting was to express optimism to an optimistic person who would not judge her seemingly misplaced attitude.

A couple of weeks later, Darla messaged me that the test results showed she had stage 4 breast cancer that had spread to her liver. However, she remained unusually positive, confident that the cancer could be treated with only a few additional weeks of chemo.

To me, this sounded worse—much worse. As a good friend, I knew this meant we had to discuss some deep, heavy stuff.

The doctors are responsible for your physical condition. Your friends can help you with your psychological condition. But a *real* friend will also be concerned about your spiritual condition.

So, I messaged her and asked her where she was spiritually, as well as what her relationship was with THE CREATOR.

She replied that she was fine, but then went on—in almost 400 words—to describe her philosophy of religion and spirituality. It included her belief in a mixture of Catholicism, tribal customs, and personal philosophies. She had created her own personal religion with a standard she was confident she was meeting.

I was still concerned. If she had just told me she was fine, then the conversation would have ended there. But she had typed lots of words to convince me—and maybe herself—she was prepared for the end. She had told me she was fine physically when clearly, she was not. Now, she had told me she was also fine spiritually. She was putting up a lot of defenses to avoid facing reality.

It would not have been easy to discuss all the aspects of her discourse. That may have been the purpose: to make me go away. But I still wasn't sure. So, I gave her three questions to ask herself and then answer—but not in a message back to me.

Why? Because she doesn't answer to *me*.

The questions:

1. *When was the last time you attended mass/church?*

2. *If you did attend mass/church now, how would it make you feel?*

3. *Why do you think you would feel this way?*

I didn't tell her how to think or what to believe. However, I wanted her to consider the alternatives, expand her possibilities, and be sure about her choices.

Of course, this dialogue would take a little time. But Darla was sure she had more time, so I thought I had enough time to help her with this process.

I realize that many people reading this will disagree with my approach, finding it way too subtle. However, many *other* people reading this will say it is way too forward, believing I should have said nothing more at all. Regardless, you can judge me all you want because on these deep, heavy issues, I don't care what you think—I really don't care.

Because I don't answer to you, just as Darla doesn't answer to me.

Whenever you do something that concerns people on both sides of an issue, their viewpoints are either:

1. You did the right thing.

Or

2. You are an idiot.

I can guarantee you there is no in-between.

In this case, I'm not sure about #1—but I hope it's not #2.

If Darla followed my instructions, she would need to consider the answers to these questions herself, and I would not be involved further unless she wanted my help. But she insisted on giving me an answer to question #1, saying she had been in church a year ago for her mother's funeral.

Of course, this answer deflected the intent of the question. She also asked why I was giving her these questions in the first place, trying to make it "my" problem again.

I restated the three questions, modifying question #1 to exclude weddings and funerals. She again answered me, not herself, saying she didn't know the answer to question #1, which in her mind meant she didn't have to deal with questions #2 and #3.

I encouraged her one more time to complete the exercise, expecting there to be more dialogue between us at some point.

I did not hear back from Darla for ten days. I hoped I hadn't upset her, but I was at least expecting an update on how her treatments were progressing.

So, I sent this message late Saturday morning:

How are you doing/feeling?

That evening, I had a wonderful time at a party with relatives and friends on vacation in the mountains of Pennsylvania. It was fun and relaxing, and one of the best aspects of such a vacation is there being no cellular service. Meaning I could enjoy the entire evening without distractions and, most importantly, without the chance of heart-wrenching news.

Late that night, when I returned to my Wi-Fi-connected residence, I noticed that Darla had not responded to my message.

However, her photos were all over my Facebook feed, with touching tributes from her daughter and friends.

The sand in her hourglass had run out quickly—much more rapidly than she had ever expected.

And just as with my friend Graham, Darla is gone—and she left this place far too soon.

And this news made me physically ill, gasping for air as all the negative emotions balled into one flaming meteor rapidly bouncing throughout my brain. I tried to process the previous five weeks in five minutes. I was angry for a moment at THE CREATOR for not giving me more time to reach her. But the reality is that if more time would have worked, then more time would have been granted.

And I can still hear her laugh... That delightful laugh...

I never imagined that I would be sharing those three questions publicly. Initially, it was close, personal communication only intended between Darla and me.

However, if you need to ask yourself these questions, please do.

But if you believe you have lots of time...

Addendum: Six months later, a lead actress on a Netflix miniseries I watched bore an uncanny resemblance to

Darla. It was difficult for me to watch, but I did. There were a couple times when the woman made certain vibrant facial expressions that made me pause the show and weep.

If only there were a pause button for life.

*Out of respect for her and her family, I have used a pseudonym in place of her real name.

WHAT NOT TO SAY TO GRIEVING PEOPLE

Death is the hardest part of life. Not only for the person, but especially for the friends and loved ones left behind. The irony is that the body in the casket feels no sorrow, yet some at the funeral are bawling their eyes out.

Reacting to the death of others is painful. When it is someone close to us, the agony is so potent, we give it a special name: grief.

Grief is one of the most complex elements of the human psyche. It impacts us in ways psychologists still cannot fully understand. This suffering is difficult to interpret because we all grieve differently. The timing, the intensity, the mixing of complex emotions all varies. It's hard to describe and is unpredictable.

I've wailed—not just cried but wailed—only once in my entire life. I had just finished all the paperwork in the nursing facility where my mother died.

As I walked down the hall past her old room for the last time, I felt this rage of emotion bubbling deep within me.

I sped up my pace, through the lobby, out the door until I was trotting across the parking lot.

I made it to my car, shut the door, and wailed.

Wailed loud. Wailed hard. Wailed long.

And the most important thing I learned from this experience is that you *must* grieve. If you don't properly grieve, it's as if you unknowingly swallow a poison pill, and the poison stays within you, inflicting all sorts of pain and creating problems in your life while you wonder and stress about where this damage could have possibly come from.

The only way to expel the poison from your soul is to let yourself grieve.

Grieving hurts, but it must occur. And we often encounter friends and associates who have suffered a great loss, such as the unexpected death of a spouse or child. We know they are in pain, and we feel the need to comfort them. So, we search for something positive to say in this horrible, terrible time.

However, we are uncomfortable around people who are grieving. This puts us under an enormous amount of stress. We need to say *something*, but because of the pressure, we don't search for the right thing to say, and we subsequently blurt out whatever thought or cliché pops into our minds. We want to say something reassuring and encouraging, but we often end up— unintentionally, I must emphasize—saying the wrong things to these people who are going through some of the most difficult trials of their lives.

In other words, if we are not careful, our comments can actually be more hurtful than helpful.

The danger here is that the grieving person is trapped in a fiery circle of distress. They have just lost a spouse, a parent, a child, a best friend, a lover, or someone else near and dear to them. They are not thinking clearly; they are not responding normally; they are not fully functioning; they are just hurting. Therefore, be extremely careful what you say to them when they are in this vulnerable state.

This subject was already on my list of future *Deep, Heavy Stuff* topics when I recently overheard my friend Theresa discussing this very issue with another friend of hers. Theresa had lost her daughter several years ago to acute lymphoblastic leukemia. After I joined the conversation, Theresa agreed to share her feelings on the topic if I called her later. On the call, she provided me with a few examples of the wrong things to say, which she quoted off the top of her head because she has heard them so often.

Here are a few examples about what not to say:

"GOD DOESN'T GIVE YOU MORE THAN YOU CAN HANDLE."

(and, similarly:

"God must have thought you were strong enough to handle this.")

What's wrong here:

You might be a person of faith, but right now, this grieving person has some serious issues, questions, and doubts about THE CREATOR. At this time, they are not very happy with THE CREATOR. The person doesn't want—nor need—to hear your "pop theology". You are most likely not a pastor or counselor, so steer clear of this road.

Also avoid: "*Everything happens for a reason.*" Because in these cases, no, there *is* no good reason. There is *never* a good reason for the loss of a loved one, and even if there was, now is not the time to inform the grieving family member or friend. So, no.

"SHE'S IN A BETTER PLACE."

(and

"*They are always with you.*")

What's wrong here:

Even if these statements can be considered true in a sense, they provide little comfort to the person.

The departed loved one is *not* physically here. The grieving person has suffered a loss, resulting in something being gone from their life. There is a tremendous void.

These statements imply that the void doesn't matter when it is actually the most painful part of the ordeal. So, once more, no.

"I KNOW HOW YOU FEEL."

(and

"Time will ease your pain."

and

"You can move on now.")

What's wrong here:

Unless you have suffered something equally traumatic, you can't possibly know how this person feels at this moment. If you have actually been traumatized this much, you probably already know not to say this. But even if you have suffered something similar, the person's grief may still be different, perhaps much more intense, than yours, simply because *everyone experiences grief differently*. The truth is you don't "know how they feel". So, again, no.

The fact that time may "heal all wounds"—and the person will eventually move on—offers no comfort in the present. Like above, even if this sentiment is technically true, it's totally irrelevant to a person currently in intense pain.

Theresa once told me, "There were times after hearing the same statement for the umpteenth time that I felt like punching the person in the face."

The purpose of this essay is not to chastise you for making these statements. We have all said the wrong thing to the wrong person at the wrong time. However, we also have the capability to learn once our mistakes have been pointed out, and we should take the opportunity to improve ourselves when we can. The reason to discuss this deep, heavy stuff is to help you next time you encounter someone in severe grief.

Please remember to think before you speak so you can avoid these misleading sentiments and console your friends and loved ones in the most respectful way possible.

WHAT TO SAY TO (AND DO FOR) GRIEVING PEOPLE

In the last essay, we looked at *what not to say* to someone who's grieving the death of a close loved one. But you do need to say something, so here's *what you should say*.

Why is this important? The grieving person is in extreme emotional pain and needs to be treated with gentleness and kindness. So no matter what, communication needs to be respectful and compassionate.

Imagine you are talking to someone lying in a hospital bed with third-degree burns. They are entirely bandaged up and looking at you through a space in the gauze. The grieving person is in as much emotional agony as this patient is in physical agony. Treat them accordingly.

RULE #1: DO NOT SAY A LOT. LET YOUR WORDS BE FEW.

For emphasis:

DO NOT SAY A LOT. LET YOUR WORDS BE FEW.

The more you talk, the more likely you are to drift into the "things not to say" category.

Think before you speak and keep your words at a minimum. No more than eight to ten words at a time are needed. And this goes for follow-up statements as well. Every statement you make should be concise and to the point.

The reason you do not need many words, to paraphrase Woody Allen: *80% of your caring is just showing up.* It's your *presence* that's important, not your words. You are *being there* for them. That's enough.

RULE #2: IT IS NOT YOUR RESPONSIBILITY OR PURPOSE TO MAKE THE GRIEVING PERSON FEEL BETTER WITH YOUR WORDS.

This rule is difficult for us positive and compassionate types to follow. As my good friend Lynn pointed out after discussing this subject, "There isn't a d@mn thing you can say that will make a grieving person feel better."

And in trying to lift the person's spirits, you risk the unintended outcomes detailed in the previous essay. At that moment, *the grieving person is not supposed to feel better; they are just supposed to grieve.* And grieving involves pain. So even though you are tempted to say positive things... No! Just no.

RULE #3: BE KIND, COMPASSIONATE, AND SOMBER.

Yes, this is common sense. But sometimes, common sense isn't as common as you think, and it's always best to have three rules.

The best thing to say, according to my friend Theresa from the previous essay, as well as people commenting on the previous essay's respective blog post, is:

"I'm sorry for your loss."

Five words. Shows sorrow and communicates caring and empathy. You are not apologizing; this statement has become the shortened version of, "I'm sorrowful for your loss."

You can also raise the intensity with: "I'm so sorry for your loss."

Or, using even fewer words:

"My condolences."

The word *condolences* is a substitute for the verb form of sympathy. In other words, you are expressing sorrow for their loss.

"My deepest condolences" takes it up a notch.

"My deepest sympathies" also works if you deem *condolences* too formal.

THE REST OF THE CONVERSATION

After expressing your sorrow, let the other person speak.

Respond by agreeing with what they said.

Nod a lot.

If appropriate, a hug or a hand on the shoulder helps convey that you care.

But the most important thing is to keep your words limited and on track. No advice, platitudes, or anything else from the previous essay.

BUT YOU'RE NOT DONE YET

Theresa (who had lost her daughter to an aggressive cancer) emphasized that highly traumatized people need special care after the tragedy.

"There's 200 people at the funeral, then nobody calls afterward," she bemoaned.

Her advice:

- Don't ignore them.
- Don't turn your back on them.
- Knock on their door with flowers.
- Invite them out for coffee or lunch.
- Hug them when you see them.

If you are a close friend, you have a responsibility to help the person through the grieving process. This is difficult because as humans, we attempt to avoid people who have suffered loss. We feel uncomfortable and awkward; we never know what to say.

I failed at this years ago with a coworker who suddenly and tragically lost his wife due to a rapidly invasive cancer. When he returned to work after several months, I knew I should say something but didn't, due to the factors above.

But that was wrong. I needed to say something. I needed to express condolences, and I never did (I did try to contact him and apologize after writing this essay, it's been 10 years since I've seen him, but he did not respond).

Coffee Talk

You can say more when you meet the person for coffee, lunch, or wherever down the road. But many of the same rules still apply: Let them talk, and you listen. They may spiritually bleed all over the table, and that's okay. It's part of the grieving process. But you are *there*, and that's more important than anything.

From Theresa: "Be kind, be compassionate."

Do not tell them how to grieve because we all grieve differently, and the amount of time needed to process our grief greatly varies. You can make positive statements at this time, but they must be short and tailored to the individual person.

And you will have to initiate these meetings. The grieving person will not reach out because they hurt too much. This is on you. You will resist doing it, BUT IT MUST BE DONE. It is YOUR responsibility as a friend.

Two More Things

Don't be afraid to say the deceased's name. Theresa said the following, and my good friend Vicki, who had lost her adult daughter, also agrees:

"What bothers me is when people grimace or move away when I mention [the deceased]—and this can be friends and family."

Also, both women emphasized that time does *not* heal this wound. It is so deep that it never goes away. Therefore, treat these people with special care.

Always.

The End

This is the deepest, heaviest stuff there is. Now you know *what to say*, as well as *what not to say* to a grieving person.

And if you are that grieving person, I hope you realize that people say stupid things under stress, and I hope you forgive and extend grace to them anyway.

I wish you peace.

WHEN A DOG DIES

When a dog dies....

January 2022 was a brutal month for my pet-loving friends, as several beloved companions had crossed the rainbow bridge. January 18th was an especially sorrowful day, with two good friends saying goodbye to their old dogs forever. One of these was a service dog who had been a faithful and dutiful helper for 14 years. The other was a beloved companion to a woman who has suffered several hardships over the past couple of years.

The timing of these hit home for me. My one and only dog passed away on the same week in 2018. Until then, I never realized what happens when a dog dies.

When a dog dies...

You do not own a dog. You form a relationship. And the dog understands it is a relationship as well. As much as you love your dog, be assured he loves you more. Because while the dog is a part of your life, you are the dog's life. You are everything to that dog. To your dog, you are a god. You feed him, you play with him, you spend time together, and you care for his every need. In your dog's eyes, you certainly are a supreme being.

This is why your dog greets you so enthusiastically when you return home or reenter a room. Your dog is special to you because no one in the world is happier to see you than your dog. My daughter's dog Lily rips around the house and barks loudly when I visit. And I'm not even her owner! She pounces on my lap and eagerly tries to kiss me as soon as I sit down. I should have been this popular back in high school.

This is why the dog is happy to see you. It's why the dog shows you such affection. It's why the dog studies your patterns and actions and conforms to your lifestyle as much as he can. The dog seeks to form a strong bond with you. It may be even more potent than a human bond. Lovers may bond more strongly at the beginning of a relationship, but the strength of that bond usually mellows over time. The bond between dog and human, on the other hand, never stops growing.

From the human side, the dog is better than any friend. He will not abandon you, even when it seems everyone else has. He is always happy to see you. On those dreadful days when you've been yelled at, lied to, backstabbed, hated, etc., your dog merely wants to lick your face. Dogs know when you are struggling, when you are down, when you are ill. That's because they have been intently watching your expressions, routines, and movements—all to love and respond to you better.

When a dog dies...

You can't understand what a person experiences when their dog passes until you experience it yourself. Before I had a dog, when someone's dog had died, I knew they were sad because they no longer had a pet. I understood sadness, and I understood pets, so I understood what was happening, right?

Not even close.

It's typically a more profound pain than the death of a cat. I have experienced both. Now, this is not to create competition or spur arguments. Dogs have the ability to bond with their humans more deeply than other pets. Therefore, the pain of separation is more intense. Some exceptional cats bond with their owners in extraordinary ways—in those cases, I imagine the grief is similar.

So in most cases, cat owners, take your grief level and turn it up a notch to know what it's like when a dog dies.

When a dog dies...

The grieving process for a dyog can take months. I was crushed when my dog died. I don't know how long it took the pain to stop. I do know that three months afterwards, I was sitting alone in the Indianapolis Airport waiting to go home. I was still grieving my dog's death and had just received some bad news about another matter.

As I sat there distressed, I was interrupted by the service dog they walk around to help people who are... well, in distress.

"Are you okay?" the handler inquired.

I reached down and patted the dog on the head as he looked at me soulfully.

"I'm okay," I replied. "But I do feel better now."

When a dog dies...

The bond between dog and human is one of the greatest joys in life. It brings happiness to the human, and we can't even imagine what the dog experiences. The bond grows so intense that the dog is not just an external being—the dog becomes part of you.

But when a dog dies, that part gets ripped away. You lose a piece of your soul that you can never get back. And that's what creates the agony, hurt, and grief.

When a dog dies...

It takes a long time to recover. Peace to all those who have lost their four-legged friends.

Chapter 9:
'Cause You Gotta Have Faith

I contend that every person has faith in something—or many things—because we are all "faithful creatures". After exploring the concept of faith in general, I share a painful personal story as well as how it can be applied in your own life. Faith is deep, heavy stuff—perhaps some of the deepest, heaviest stuff of all.

Even the "Faithless" Have Faith

We are all faithful creatures—everyone has faith in something.

Everyone has faith in something. Even atheists have faith. They have faith in atheism, and they may have more faith than you do—just in something that may not be considered "traditional" to have faith in. And everyone has doubts, although agnostics may have more of it.

But agnostics have faith, too, because:

We are all faithful creatures—everyone has faith in something.

But where did this inherent desire to have faith, place faith, or feel faith come from? It is indeed a complex concept, part of our human psyche. It can't be seen, yet it is ingrained in everyone.

We were either created by a supreme being who designed us so we would have the capacity to have faith in that supreme being, or...

We evolved with a need to have faith in something, and that need was so strong that we have created mythical beings whose purpose is to be a receptacle for the faith we exude. This would indicate that faith serves some survival benefit which hasn't yet been discovered. Much of it may be purely psychological.

Either way, it would suggest that our need to place our faith in something is fundamentally forceful, which means:

We are all faithful creatures—everyone has faith in something.

We know that faith is the component that connects us to—or disconnects us from—a belief in a deity. Faith (or a variation of the word) appears 458 times in THE BOOK, and in almost every section of the NEW BOOK. Based on THE BOOK, faith is collectively described as one of the most potent forces in our lives.

Regarding belief in a supreme being, faith is essential because you cannot prove THE CREATOR exists. It must be accepted by faith, and the amount of faith you possess is important. Your belief can be supported by logic, but it still must be based on faith.

However, you cannot prove THE CREATOR doesn't exist, either. So, if you have no faith in a supreme being, you might have great faith in science instead, especially to believe in evolution. Therefore, some atheists have lots more faith than members of the church choir. It takes just as much faith (if not more, according to my pastor friend Mike) to believe in evolution as it does in creation.

However, it does take more effort to believe in a deity. Non-belief, by its nature, is usually more passive. Of course, some will claim that this extra effort is proof there is no deity, but others will argue that the absence of effort is the reason for the skepticism.

You can even narrow the gap if you define this debate as being between "those who believe in science" and "those who believe in the one who created the science". Just don't try the "but science is perfect" argument here because in this context, it loses some of its substance. And because no one has the answer, we should continue to seek out the truth and each work out our faith.

Because:

We are all faithful creatures—everyone has faith in something.

THE BOOK defines faith as: having the confidence that things you are hoping for will happen and having the conviction that things you cannot see are, in fact, real.

And this definition is not limited to things in the highly spiritual realm; it confirms that humans are faithful creatures, in need of having faith in something.

We are all faithful creatures—everyone has faith in something.

The critical issue: Our innate drive to be full of faith causes us to put our faith in many things, such as money, possessions, people, politicians, jobs, lovers, movements, ideas, the Earth, sports teams, humankind, and so on. Having faith in something gives us comfort, happiness, contentment, calmness, and it helps us sleep at night. I guess this is a possible evolutionary reason for being faithful, even if it doesn't explain how it got into us.

Of course, the problem with putting our faith in any of these earthly things is that ultimately, they all will let us down. They will fail, often when we need them the most. Not one is truly worthy of our faith, no matter how strong our faith is in them. The betrayal, disappointment, sadness, discouragement, and depression we feel afterwards can more than offset those psychological benefits of having faith in the first place.

In what you place your faith is THE BIG QUESTION. Therefore, it requires focused consideration and is a life-long journey. Do not be flippant about your choices or let other people make those decisions for you.

One more thing: Just like how there is nothing wrong with having faith, there is nothing wrong with having doubt as well. There is faith as well as doubt among everyone. If faith is the absence of doubt, then everyone has some faith, and everyone has some doubt—there is just a difference in how much and where it's placed. So, shouldn't everyone continue to seek the truth and then decide where to place their faith?

THE CONCLUSION:

We are all faithful creatures – everyone has faith in something.

If we all realize we are all faithful beings, we can be less judgmental and discuss our differences cordially. That's it. Period. Full stop. That's all she wrote.

And another note: Regardless of what turns out to be the truth, it's still much better to place your faith in something intrinsically good than in nothing at all.

A WORD ABOUT RELIGION

If religion is "man's attempt to get to God", then every religion will have corruption, abuse, fraud, dishonesty, etc. Religion, ironically, is the best example of mankind's failings. If men are not capable of maintaining holiness, no matter the institution, then what hope is there in any religion? This also makes a good argument for rejecting all religion—at least all *organized* religion.

So we must accept that religion will not get you to whatever deity you are trying to reach. Unfortunately, this means we must get there despite the religious practices, customs, dogma, and—yes—corruption. Many people reject the total because of the actions of a few. Faith is strictly a personal belief, just between you and THE CREATOR or whatever spirit in the cosmos you are trying to find.

You can't depend on your "group", sect, religious affiliation, or denomination to get you there. Only yourself.

This means you must do the work to figure it out. And it's a journey, not an event, revelation, or epiphany. It's a process, and due to the previously mentioned doubts, it should be a life-long journey.

In our culture, some believe we should be able to customize our religion, taking the best of all faiths and combining it into the best thing for us. But by doing this, you create our own personalized god. And in practice, you will be able to rationalize every action because your god is basically yourself.

You may believe our culture is becoming less religious, but it's not. Brand new religions are springing forth all over. These new religions are based on beliefs about ideas, concepts, personal behaviors, the environment, and so on. They each have their own dogmas, ceremonies, creeds, chants, and so on. The way they shun people for heresy would put the Puritans to shame. Their enforcement of adherence could even be considered cultish.

So as devotion to THE CREATOR diminishes, new idols emerge. Why?

   We are all faithful creatures—everyone has faith in something.

To fill the void left by monotheism, you get polytheism. If you think this is a good thing or has never occurred before, I will refer you to the OLD BOOK. We are in danger of making a most ominous trade.

The last bit of advice I will offer is this:

Do not reject THE MAN based solely on the imperfect actions of His followers. If you truly seek, then you will find.

THE DOOR

Knock, and the door will be opened to you...

A simple statement by THE MAN. But is it a command? A suggestion? A promise, perhaps?

The words are so basic that almost all translations of the original text are identical:

Knock, and the door will be opened to you...

However, like many statements from THE MAN, it is simple and yet frustratingly complex, not wholly understood by even the wisest, most intelligent human minds.

Regardless, some years ago, a person I love faced a challenge. I did not believe it would be a tough challenge, but it was a big step for her. So, if the instruction is, *"Knock, and the door will be opened to you"...*

I knocked.

And it initially seemed as if the request would be promptly answered, and the door opened.

But just as quickly as the door was opened, it slammed shut. It was a false hope, appearing as a cruel trick.

We were back to square one, so I knocked again.

But disappointingly, there was no progress. There was no answer. None. It seemed as if no one was home.

What's wrong? *"Knock, and the door will be opened to you"*...

I'm knocking. No one is opening.

In our flawed perspective, we interpret the statement as: *"knock once, and the door will immediately swing open wide"*. But it doesn't say "knock once", and it also doesn't say "knock gently".

I knocked.

I knocked.

I knocked some more.

I kept knocking.

Nothing.

This was highly frustrating because this was a situation where the longer it took to succeed, the harder success became. The pressure built, and so did my agitation.

A year went by, and the door remained shut. But I continued to knock.

The repeatedly unanswered petitions generated doubt. My request was good and pure and noble, and it wasn't even for me. There was no good reason why this was taking so long. This whole thing should have been over by now. I could not understand why the door remained shut. The longer this went on, the more doubts there were, yet I knocked again.

After three years of knocking, there was some progress that generated much hope. I could feel the door loosening. There was a small crack, and perhaps it would open soon.

But then, there was a setback. The door quickly shut, and the lock securely clicked in place.

I stared at the door in disgust. Hope had been vanquished once again. I was crushed.

And yet, I knocked. I wondered what I lacked; in that I was knocking but the door was not opening as stated. But what I did not lack was faith. The act of continuing to knock—even when there is no answer—is a sign of substantial faith. You only continue to knock on a door when you believe someone is home. I knew someone was home, yet there was no answer, and the door remained shut.

The knocking continued for years. However, as the frustration grew, the knocks became pounds and then, as desperation set in, the pounds became two-fisted strikes accompanied by yelling.

"Are you listening?! Can you hear me?! Do you not see what is happening here?!"

It says "knock". It does not say "beg". But mere knocking wasn't working, so I begged for the door to be opened. But the result was the same.

And then, there was progress again. Hope returned. The door had cracked open. I then did everything in my power to open that door. I ran and slammed against it with all my might. I pushed with all my strength. Trying so hard and failing was painful and exhausting.

Despite my efforts, the door would not open. It would not even budge an inch. Unfortunately, in this circumstance, partial success meant that total success was unlikely. There were now added barriers to getting the door open.

The next time I approached the door, there were steel bars across it, and huge locks were wrapped around the doorknob. This door would not and could not be opened. I had tried everything to get the door open, but now, the new circumstances had made it impossible.

It forced me to reevaluate the situation. The person most affected by the current state of things was happy. Everyone else involved was happy, too. Therefore, I decided that I would be satisfied with a partial victory. It wasn't the outcome I desired, but it was a better situation than when it began. I would settle with what we had. I would come to peace with the circumstances.

And... I would stop knocking.

Accepting this outcome was a process that took some time. After knocking for over eight years, settling doesn't come quickly. Eventually, I was able to accept the outcome and be at peace. It felt good not having to knock anymore and being free of the resulting worries and frustrations.

But then, disaster struck. A terrible, unfortunate mistake was made which caused the entire structure to come crashing down in an instant.

The damage was massive. There was no fixing this. And there were consequences to this tragedy.

I was devasted. I was distraught. I was distressed. It hurt bad, and it hurt deeply. It was one of those all-encompassing emotional pains that you cannot shake. I was angry at all parties that had caused this mess. And I could not understand why, after working so hard to accept the situation, it had suddenly disintegrated.

I was in persistent agony for two days. Rolling the details around in my head in a torturous loop.

As I surveyed the damage, I noticed that the impenetrable door, with all its locks and bars, had been ripped off its hinges and now was just a pile of waste. This disaster had destroyed the building, but now, that door was no longer an impediment. I looked at the broken door, so uncertain about the future.

Then, I heard a voice say: *Turn around.*

There stood an entirely different house. The game had changed but the barrier remained. I walked over to the door, very much like the original one, except with no steel bars or heavy locks. I stared at the door, as I had an important choice to make. This is the acid test of faith.

It's easy to walk away at this point. It may even be logical to walk away. However, faith is not easy—nor is it logical.

It's just faith, or it isn't.

Circumstances change.

People change.

Everything in this world changes except...

Knock, and the door will be opened to you...

So, I knocked, and I knocked again. And kept knocking for another nine months.

Until, finally, the door swung open. Just like I had expected it to nearly ten years ago.

Knock, and the door will be opened to you...

And keep knocking. No matter what, keep knocking.

FAITH IS DEEP, HEAVY STUFF

I detailed my struggles with faith in the previous allegory, "The Door", which admittedly was embarrassing to write. The purpose of the story is not to hold me up as some "super-spiritual" being. If anything, it shows that I am a "super-stubborn" being, which I will gladly confirm.

I wrote the story to show that faith is difficult and often painful. That doubts are normal and even can be signs of faith themselves. And that sometimes, persistence is what ultimately opens the door.

How does it feel to get your answer after praying for something for ten years? You are as jubilant as you may think. It's like fighting a long war. Even if you win, the greatest comfort is knowing that the conflict has ended, not so much the victory obtained. And in this case, I still had to wait several months to be sure the answer would hold.

Yes, the fact that my prayer was answered did strengthen my faith in THE CREATOR, but it also produced doubt in myself. Why did it take so long? What is my status when it comes to faith?

And this "faith" thing is probably the most mysterious aspect of this particular spiritual realm. I'm sensing that no one truly understands it. If some guru says they do, they are lying. It may be the deepest, heaviest stuff there is.

Faith is so complex that no one can understand it. However, you benefit in doing the puzzle—not from solving it, but from putting in the effort.

THERE ARE LEVELS OF FAITH

A reexamination of THE MAN's proclamation of:

"Truly I tell you, if you have faith as small as a mustard seed, you can say to this mountain, 'Move from here to there,' and it will move. Nothing will be impossible for you."***

First of all, this is totally figurative in nature. Faith will not give you telekinesis.

What this statement does is contrast one of the smallest things the people were familiar with—a mustard seed, about .05 inches in diameter—to one of the largest: a mountain.

This passage is almost always regarded in positive terms: *Wow! You only need a tiny amount of faith to do great things! So, get out there and move some mountains!* However, in context, this is not an affirmation but a condemnation.

THE MAN is explaining to, maybe even admonishing, his cohorts why they couldn't accomplish the task at hand. The entire passage reads:

He replied, "<u>Because you have so little faith.</u> Truly I tell you, if you have faith as small as a mustard seed, you can say to this mountain, 'Move from here to there,' and it will move. Nothing will be impossible for you."

So, the answer to my question of "Why did it take nearly ten years to accomplish a very reasonable outcome?" is precisely the same:

"Because you have so little faith."

But now I understand that this was not the right question to ask. *Because faith is not static.* Perhaps it is like the stock market, in that as you buy into THE CREATOR using thoughts, prayers, and deeds, your faith increases. When you sell out those concepts, your level of faith falls.

In other words: You get what you put into it.

Most of us overestimate our amount of faith. We compare our faith with that of others. If we perceive our faith to be greater than most, we deem it sufficient. We then justify there being no need for change, and we sleep well at night. However, that is a faulty scale.

The gold standard, though, remains this:

"Truly I tell you, if you have faith as small as a mustard seed, you can say to this mountain, 'Move from here to there,' and it will move. Nothing will be impossible for you."

You may believe your faith is sufficient. That it must be bigger than the proverbial mustard seed. But consider: How many mountains have you moved recently? How many mountains have you moved in your entire life?

But even so, we can't give up, right? Because our faith is not static. You always have the opportunity to build your faith, and when you do, some mountains move. Because the statement above is either true, or it's not.

My question resulting from "The Door" is not:

"Why did it take ten years to get an answer?"

But something much deeper and heavier...

"Why was this prayer answered at that point in time? Or maybe, why was it answered at all?"

Well, in "The Door", I talk about the devastating effects that happened around the end of year eight. Unfortunately, I must keep the details private, hence the story being intentionally vague. However, a mistake was made that had horrible consequences and severely damaged the process.

Yet despite the horrible results of this action, I was somehow able to see the one flicker of hope it had provided. In the 99% of darkness, I was able to see the 1% of light. And I acted quickly and forcefully. If you need a working definition of faith that you can understand, there you go. Take the flicker and run with it!

At that moment, my amount of faith went from *smaller than a mustard seed* to being at least *equal to a mustard seed*. Several months later, the door swung wide open. I was astounded at how easily the mountain moved.

But don't think for a moment that I have this all figured out. I still have mountains that I want to move. I just need a few more mustard seeds.

'* Hebrews 11:1

'** Matthew 7:7

'*** Matthew 17:20

CHAPTER 10:
HATE IS A DESTRUCTIVE FORCE

Most wars are fought and most murders are committed because of hate. Outward expressions of hatred are always destructive in some manner. However, inward manifestations of hate are also damaging to our bodies and souls. Hate is a poison that we manufacture inside of us. If left to fester, bad things inevitably follow.

Dealing with hate is deep, heavy stuff. In this chapter, there is a warning about the amount of hate generated in our culture and how to resist it. Then, a personal story (or two) about dealing with those who have harmed us. And finally, some thoughts about forgiveness.

DON'T BE A HATER

The combination of social media and 24-hour cable news has created a culture of hate. It is poisoning us as we take it in, one drip at a time, day after day. And the politicians—on *both* sides—have learned how to use this to their advantage.

The game is to separate us into teams—"us" versus "them"—and then encourage *us* to hate *them*. There is a basic human desire to identify with a team or "tribe"; this is why there are so many sports fans. But these "tribes" are now based on skin color, social class, political party, religion, or opinions (including lack thereof) on important issues. Notably, during the pandemic, these were also "teams" regarding the use of masks and vaccines; instead of "shirts vs. skins", there was "masks vs. mouths".

It is so easy to get pushed onto a "team" when people hurl hateful statements and accusations your way. And once you identify with a team, it is natural to begin hating the "other" team, no matter who they are or what other beliefs they may hold.

In other words, it is now culturally acceptable to hate people—people who you have never met and most likely never will. You would have been considered mentally ill if you publicly showed this much hatred toward anybody 20 years ago. But today, there are so many repositories to spill your hate, with the vilest tweets and comments encouraged and praised.

This means our culture becomes more hateful every day. Hate is evil. By extension, this means our culture becomes more *evil* every day. And we can see that evil on the nightly news with people beaten or shot randomly by total strangers.

You get tricked into saying:

"THOSE people over there! Look at what they're doing! Listen to the awful things they're saying!"

But "those people" may be saying the exact same thing about you, regardless of whether you've actually said or done anything "awful". You may see yourself as being on the "us" team, but at the same time, you are someone else's "them". And what do you do then? *You can't control what others are thinking or doing. You are only responsible for yourself.* In this caustic environment, we need this introspection and restraint often.

It is dangerous to hate your so-called "enemies". Taken to the extreme, you will want to kill all your enemies to achieve what you believe is good. We sometimes hear comments like these expressed by people on television and online with minimal shock and repulsion. Is it surprising that gun sales continue to flourish?

It becomes harder to resist joining the haters every day. Evil people are at work generating enemies for you. Recently, a commentary argued that hating groups of Americans is fine since "people have always hated others." This fellow must really enjoy hating people. He knows it's wrong, yet he attempts to justify his hatred.

But is "there's always been hate and haters" an acceptable standard? If not, what *is* the standard?

Of course, THE MAN had something to say about this persistent, destructive human condition:

"You have heard that it was said, 'You shall love your neighbor and hate your enemy.' But I say to you, Love your enemies...."

If you think this is difficult for you reading this today, the original audience of this speech was entirely surrounded by their enemies. One group was persecuting and exploiting them, and the other wanted to kill them all. We often dismiss this command because we believe it is unattainable. But basically, what THE MAN is saying is:

The solution, antidote, remedy, etc., to the evilest destructive force in our world—*hate*—is the most potent force for good in the universe—*love*.

It is instinctive for humans to hate those who harm, oppose, or hate us. However, the people hearing this edict were not expected to ignore the persecutions or to defend themselves from being harmed. They were instructed to love their enemies despite all the hatred being thrown their way.

I have found this difficult to do in a business setting when you face and work with an adversary daily. In most cases, I did well, but I will confess that I have failed a few times, as you will see in the following essay.

At a minimum, even if we can't love our enemies, it is wrong to hate them. THE BOOK mentions "love" 686 times, and "hate" only 127 times. And I doubt any of those 127 mentions portray hate in favorable terms.

Don't let the cultural forces turn you into a hater. All the hateful people out there will claim their hate is necessary for change to occur. That their hate is expressed "for the greater good". However, there is no "greater good" than love, which includes loving your enemies. Change needs to happen, but it needs to happen in the right way. Think how much better change could be if our rulers loved each other and sought to work together for that greater good, rather than fight for power like rats fighting for cheese.

Don't let the haters turn you into a hater. If you can't love your enemies, at least show them all the grace and respect you can.

THE NEMESIS

I had a nemesis. He wasn't an enemy—we weren't actively engaged in conflict–but he was still a nemesis, someone who made me want to spit on the ground every time his name was mentioned.

I never liked Greg from the day I met him. And I never pretended to. He sensed my aversion because I couldn't hide it. In my neighborhood growing up, we were honest about our feelings toward each other: If someone didn't like you, you knew it, and vice versa. I never learned the vital skill of *pretending* to like someone, which was detrimental to my business career.

Despite my disdain for the guy, I still played nice, which is my nature. There were no direct confrontations.

But then, there was the *incident.*

Now, I am often oblivious when someone mistreats me (after all, I do my best to give people the benefit of the doubt), and I often need my friends or spouse to clue me in whenever an injustice has been leveled. That said, when Greg had risen to a powerful position in our company and took an opportunity to snuff me out (in a business sense, of course), all my friends and associates believed this was a personal, deliberate vendetta—almost like a mafia hit—and over time, I realized it as well.

The verdict became unanimous: I got shafted—shafted bad and unfairly—due to no fault of my own.

And so, I had "enmity", or the state or feeling of being actively opposed or hostile toward someone—this "someone" being Greg. There was bad blood—the baddest of blood! I had a *NEMESIS* whose act of vengeance left me with no response. I just had to deal with the unfortunate results of his attack.

Fortunately, I no longer had to see him. But other people would sometimes bring up his name in conversation, usually with disdain. Many years after the *incident*, my new coworkers would not say his name in my presence, and I would only speak his name when absolutely necessary.

EVENTUALLY CROSSING PATHS

Almost five years after the *incident*, Greg and I were at a trade show, and eventually, I spotted him at his company booth. By then, I was in a much better place and was prepared to reconcile. But before I could approach him, I sensed he was very apprehensive and uncomfortable seeing me. Of course, that made me feel extremely awkward, so I did not speak to him.

A year later, I was eating a snack at a reception for the same convention when Greg unexpectedly showed up in the same room. I hadn't had time to prepare for this encounter. I responded by panicking, wolfing down my food, and bolting for the door at the earliest opportunity.

However, knowing that my *NEMESIS* was uncomfortable in my presence provided some gratification. I imagined what I might do if we were ever forced to meet in a business setting, which remained a possibility. I thought about giving him a sinister look, the type a villain gives right before he rips somebody's heart out with his bare hands. I considered giving him a huge bear hug, thanking him for the *incident*. There would be those fearful seconds where he wouldn't know if I would release him or crush his ribs. But I wouldn't actually be thanking him, would I? Yes, I did recover splendidly from the *incident*, but then there is the matter of the ill intent. The intent was bad, so the blood remains bad.

But for the following six years, I'd never found myself in a situation where I *had* to talk to Greg. Until...

THE DINNER

Recently, I was invited by my good friend Mike to a fundraising dinner for a charity I support. I had never been to one of these, but Mike is now on the board of this organization, and he insisted I attend.

Upon arriving, my wife and I exchanged pleasantries with Mike and his wife. He told me several people would be attending that I had not seen in a while. Including...

"Hey, you know Greg Gottfried, don't you? He'll be here."

Well, of course, this wasn't a pleasantry (there was nothing "pleasant" about it!), and my smile instantly vanished. I quickly pulled Mike aside and explained the *incident* so he wouldn't try to reintroduce me to Greg later.

The seating at the dinner was preassigned. Your table number was on a registry, and your nametag by your chair. After finding our seats, I broke the startling news to my wife:

"Greg Gottfried will be here tonight."

She seemed more amused than concerned with this revelation.

Me? I was agitated. I was expecting an uplifting, pleasant evening, but now, I had to deal with this. It was a large banquet room, spaced out a little more than usual due to the pandemic. I was at the front corner of the room, and if he were sitting on the other side, I would never even see him.

"I wish I would have checked the register to see what table he's at," I told my wife.

Moments later, the register popped up on the main screen.

"He's at Table 8. It's probably way over there," I said.

"Look, it's right there!" she exclaimed.

I spun around to see a big "8" on the table directly behind us to the right. Well, there was no avoiding this predicament. It was obvious he was going to see me. As I often tell people: At 6'3" with a shaved head, I'm hard to miss.

It was then that I first asked myself the question:

What are you going to do?

My wife grabs my arm a few minutes later and whispers, "He's here."

I have to look, *and there he was, "like disgust lemon sour—I smell vex and conflict".*

My wife was so intrigued by this melodrama that I had to tell her to quit looking back at that table. She was having a great time with this, as she was getting a "dinner and a show".

But ... What are you going to do?

And I could hear the Eagles' song "Heartache Tonight" in my head. Was somebody really going to get hurt tonight before the night is done...?

REALLY – WHAT ARE YOU GOING TO DO?

It was supposed to be such a delightful evening -- the first banquet event of the post-pandemic era. A chance to see some old friends, enjoy a great meal, and learn more about a charity I had supported for years. But now, I sit only twenty feet from my *NEMESIS*—a person who had done me wrong years ago.

I know he is right over there at the table behind me, and I know he has seen me. I'm easily in his field of vision. And now my emotions are spinning, trying to figure out what to do.

What should I do? What should I do? I feel like I need to do something, but what?

I really can't punch him in the face, can I? A charity dinner does not seem like the appropriate place for a beatdown. It would put a damper on the evening for the over 200 people present—and did I mention it was for charity? It would cause problems for my friend Mike (*"Who invited that crazy guy to this lovely event, anyway?"*), and it would even cause problems for my *other* friend Mike (tip of the cap to *Newhart*), who oversaw the facilities that night and would have to clean up my mess if the fight escalated.

And I could get arrested. Oh, and I could lose my job.

I decided that a punch in the face would feel good at the time, but not for long.

However, I am still highly agitated, and I can't calm down. I'm thinking that if he does not acknowledge me, then why should I acknowledge him? I'm just going to pretend he isn't there, and we can both ignore this elephant in the room. After all, it's a banquet hall; there is plenty of room for me, him, and that darned elephant.

And that works for me. I calm down and enjoy my meal, having a great time reminiscing with some old friends at my table. Yes, ignoring my *NEMESIS* was not difficult, and doing nothing was by far the easiest thing to do.

However, in life, the easiest thing to do is seldom the right thing to do.

My wife, meanwhile, was still highly entertained by the drama, so much so that she continued to play the role of the agitator.

"He just walked right behind you," she said.

"What???" I snapped back.

"Yeah! He went up to get his dessert and walked right behind your chair."

Due to COVID, the desserts were not by your plate but on a large table in the front corner of the hall. I looked back to where my *NEMESIS* was seated, and sure enough, the shortest path between his chair and the desserts ran right behind me.

I had been snubbed. Now to most people, this would be a minor offense. But I hate being snubbed. It's a personal fault. If you ignore me, it sets me off. I know it's wrong, but unfortunately, I can't control it. So, my internal reaction to being snubbed is:

OH, NO, YOU DON'T!

If my emotions were spinning before, they were now kicked up to a higher gear. As the program for the evening started, I couldn't concentrate on anything else because once again:

Well, you just got snubbed! What will you do now?

And then the TRUTHFUL VOICE (inside my head, agnostics can refer to it as your "conscience") suddenly joined the conversation:

Me: "This has to stop! It's driving me crazy. This needs to end tonight."

Truthful Voice: Yes, this does need to end tonight. And you know how to end it, don't you?

Me: "Yes, I do know how to end it, but that ain't gonna happen. No way!"

Truthful Voice: Oh, then who's going to be the bigger man tonight?

Me: "I don't care about being the "bigger man". Even if I did do the right thing, he would still think he's the bigger man because he has an enormous ego. Why, it's bigger... bigger than ..."

Truthful Voice: Yours?

Me: "Yes, even bigger than mine! But I still don't care about being the bigger man. Not one bit. Nice try, but I ain't budging."

Truthful Voice: All right, then. Who's going to be the BETTER man?

Me: "Once again, that doesn't matter! I am so clearly the better man. This is not up for debate. If you asked 100 people who know us both, I am confident that 97% of those people would say I am the better man, and the other 3% would be wrong."

Truthful Voice: Okay, so let's say you are the better man. What would the better man do tonight?

Me: "Ohhh... Aaahh... Ehhh... Uhh... Hmm... Yes, I know the answer to that one. I guess... I could... possibly consider it ...."

Truthful Voice: That's good. Of course, if HE would happen to do the right thing before YOU do, that would make HIM the better man, wouldn't it?

Me: "OH, THAT IS NOT GOING TO HAPPEN! This is going to end tonight— as soon as I can end it!"

Truthful Voice: Thought you might see it my way ... I'm out of here ...

Me: "Well played, Truthful Voice—Inside my head—well played."

And as soon as the program ended, I walked over, smiled, and extended my hand.

The smile? No, I wasn't happy to see him. I was smiling because the better man was doing the better thing.

My *NEMESIS* was still nervous in my presence. There was no pleasant "how have you been?" chit-chat. Instead, he immediately diverted the conversation into an area of mutual, impersonal interest. We talked for a couple of minutes before someone else approached him. Strangely enough, this was the best conversation I have ever had with my *NEMESIS*.

The next day, I notified three friends—all of whom know the whole story between us—that I had shaken hands with my *NEMESIS*.

Joe, a positive guy, replied, "I'm proud of you!"

Sam's reply was a sarcastic, "Way to go! You did a great job with your restraint." Which is Sam's way of saying: *I'm glad you didn't punch him in the face.*

However, Karl's reply was not as pleasant: "Spit in your palm first?"

Now, you might think Karl was joking, but I assure you, he was not. But Karl was not alone in his disgust. Sam told me that several years ago, one of his friends encountered my *NEMESIS* in a store parking lot. That chance meeting resulted in a threat of gun violence and the police being summoned.

Now you may understand why this story is worth telling.

It's A Good Feeling To Leave The Past Behind

Somehow, I ended up doing the right thing even though I didn't want to. Maybe it's a sign of maturity. Perhaps it reflects the acquired wisdom of now knowing the right thing to do. Or it could mean that as we age, we realize it's not worth hanging on to the resentment generated by grudges from long ago.

I now have one fewer nemesis, and it feels good. Unfortunately, there are still a couple more out there somewhere. I'm not likely to ever encounter them again, but if I do, I hope I can handle it this well.

A few months later, I was with Sam and our friend Dougie. Sam asked me to tell him the handshake story. After I retold the whole event, Dougie's big grin disappeared into disbelief.

"You're a better man than I!" he proclaimed.

But this story is not about me being some great "better man". The lesson is that I *became* a better man by doing the correct, *better thing*. When faced with a difficult choice, we become "better" people by doing the right thing.

A Word About Forgiveness

Forgiveness seems like a simple concept, but it has some complexities. The command to forgive is almost entirely for our benefit. If we hold hatred for someone inside us, it damages our mental, physical, and spiritual health. Few things are this damaging to our total well-being.

You could argue that I should not have a nemesis if I had already forgiven him. However, I no longer held hatred against him, and I had not planned harm against him, so I had forgiven him in some sense. But seeing him again did kick up bad memories which had not been resolved. There still was some unfinished business.

I do not ascribe to the concept of "forgive and forget". Forgiveness, by nature, means you are no longer holding on to the hate against that person. However, it can be dangerous to forget. If the person harmed you in the past, he could repeat the action in the future.

It is impossible to forget when the perpetrator is a business rival you work with daily. Then you must defend yourself without hating the person—a most challenging task.

I would say forgiveness is:

1. Not planning or taking revenge
2. Not talking badly about the person to others
3. Not holding hate against the person in your heart
4. Being courteous to the person when interacting.

Forgiving the person does not mean you have to like them!

ONE MORE WEIRD STORY

Many years ago, I was involved in negotiations to bring a popular band to perform at our church. We had almost sealed the deal when a rival church who had heard about our plans swooped in and booked the band before us.

The person responsible for this was Gary Johnson (a poor pseudonym, but I can't remember his name). I knew who he was since he was active in the local concert scene, and maybe I had seen him once briefly on stage. However, even though I had never met Gary Johnson, I was furious with him for his transgression. This anger burned within me for over a week. I was so mad that I imagined punching him in the face as punishment for his action.

I admit, not an appropriate Christian response—but, of course, "*he started it!*"

I was still holding on to this anger as I took my usual long jog around my neighborhood. I was close to finishing up, about four blocks from home, when I spotted my neighbor Joe throwing a football with another guy. Now, Joe was also the morning deejay at the local Christian radio station.

I stopped and greeted Joe. After the usual pleasantries, Joe said, "See that guy over there?" He pointed to the guy holding the football. "That's Gary Johnson!".

I didn't see that one coming. This is like one of those surreal stories from THE OLD BOOK, with mine enemy—excuse me, *my* enemy—being delivered in my hands.

Gary Johnson had no idea who I was. I could have walked right up to him and sucker-punched him hard. He would have had no idea who hit him and why. Of course, I would have informed him why he was bleeding before leaving.

But this didn't happen because I was scared out of my wits by this occurrence. I quickly said goodbye to Joe and jogged—maybe sprinted—home without even acknowledging Gary Johnson.

Of course, the TRUTHFUL VOICE (Inside my head) can't let this one go:

Truthful Voice: I thought you wanted to punch Gary Johnson in the face? He was right there.

Me: "No, I changed my mind. We're all good here."

Lesson: Don't harbor enmity against your neighbor. And be careful what you wish for – you might just get it!

'* Matthew 5:43-44

CHAPTER 11: PERSONAL TRAITS FOR A RICHER LIFE

On the surface, this chapter is all about simple behaviors that we all agree we should do. However, we have forgotten these basic truths, and as our culture deteriorates, they get pushed out of view. It is not a surprise that few if any of these traits are expressed on social media.

So consider this to be a friendly reminder regarding politeness, kindness, appreciation, civility, and empathy. We all know these are what we *should* have, but making life changes in these areas? That's some deep, heavy stuff.

PLEASE READ THIS... THANK YOU ...

My elderly mother was in a hospital bed soon after a near-fatal heart attack. We talked a bit when I first arrived, but she had grown weary, and now her eyes were closed as she struggled for every breath. I sat in silence, watching her breathe, wondering if one of those would be her last, hoping she had not come to the end of the line.

Suddenly, the evening nurse burst through the door. There was a quick greeting, then the nurse checked my mother's vitals and began servicing the room. This woman was meticulous and dedicated to her job. There was no idle chit-chat because she was working so diligently. I presumed it had been a tough day since she appeared glum. Maybe she was behind on her rounds, hence the rapid work pace. My mother returned to her restive state soon after her vitals were completed.

As I sat there, I appreciated how hard this nurse worked to ensure my mother and her room were cared for. I felt the need to thank her for her effort before she bolted out the door to her next room. I patiently waited as she completed her tasks and turned to go.

The words "thank you" were right on my lips when my mother opened her eyes and said:

"Thank you."

And when my mother said "thank you" to anyone, her tone and facial expression denoted a deep appreciation. It wasn't lip service. It was more as if she had bestowed a blessing upon you.

Yes, I did thank the nurse as well, but my words paled compared to my mother's response.

My mother was extremely polite, and of course, she raised me to be the same. However, even though people would say I am polite, I am not nearly as polite as my mother. And most of us would agree that we were also raised to be polite, yet we often fail to be. So, we KNOW we should say "please" and "thank you" routinely, yet many of us DO NOT. It is the most glaring gap between head knowledge and actual behavior in our society. Unfortunately, as our culture becomes more rude and demanding, it also becomes much less polite.

Therefore:

- Even though your mother told you this...
- Even though you already know you *should* do this...
- Even though you already know *how* to do this...

PLEASE SAY "PLEASE" AND "THANK YOU" at every appropriate opportunity!

BUSINESS APPLICATIONS

One area where politeness has diminished is in the corporate world (I have a friend who does workshops on "Business Etiquette", otherwise known as "telling grown adults who already *know* how to act appropriately to actually *do* it"). Companies are plagued with people demanding, insisting, and ordering their workers to perform.

So, a word to all supervisors, bosses, managers, and executives: These people are not your slaves—they are literally your coworkers in achieving your organization's success and serving your customers and clients. Therefore, some respect, please! A "please" for every request and a "thank you" when it is completed.

This is simple. This is basic. And it will improve your ability to manage people and projects as well as your company's performance.

And remember: *How you treat your employees determines how your employees treat your customers!*

REAL APPLICATION

Lately, I have been trying to include "Please" in every email which requests something. This is a small detail that is easy to omit. Think otherwise? Go back and look at the last five request emails you sent, and you will likely be disappointed. One of my email catchphrases is: "*Just let me know*". It should always be: "*Please let me know*".

"But Don, if nobody else is doing this, why should I?"

Because you can't change the whole world, only *your* world. By being less demanding and more polite, you can improve the mood and outlook of everyone you encounter. If it makes you feel good when someone is polite to you, well, then, y'know...

As your mother once said, "It isn't that difficult."

And a side note to you young guys out there: Being polite makes you more attractive to women who have been raised to be polite, as they will likely value politeness in a possible suitor. It can give you an advantage over guys with superior attributes or resources. Not to mention polite wives are easier to live with than demanding ones (*Just sayin'!*).

Being polite and saying "please" and "thank you" gives you an advantage in business, relationships, and in life. No other simple, free thing can benefit your life in so many ways.

CONSIDER THIS A FRIENDLY REMINDER

Please try to say and write "please" and "thank you" more often this week and see how much better it feels and how it improves the way people respond to you. Your mother will be—or would have been—pleased by this. And she would also be happy with me for reminding you.

And, oh yes, I almost forgot ... Thank you for reading this!

AND SMILE MORE!

One of my mother's most endearing traits was her smile. Whenever she saw someone, including me, she would immediately break out into a full smile, nonverbally expressing, "*I'm so glad to see you!*"

And not surprisingly, everyone loved my mom.

I believe she learned this behavior from her father, who owned a neighborhood grocery store for many years. Whenever he saw a customer he knew (and he knew many of them), he would smile and wave. My mother worked in his store at a young age and learned to imitate this behavior.

We would all benefit from smiling more. It improves relationships. It enhances what people think of you. It brightens your outlook on life. It diffuses tense situations. It is tremendously effective in the business world, especially when dealing with clients and bosses (many of whom often create the aforementioned "tense situations"). And if you are single, it makes you more appealing to whomever you are seeking to attract.

I admit I need to work on this. I am not skilled at appearing happy when I'm not—of course, there are some people you aren't really pleased to see. So, this will have to be a learned behavior, which at my age is more difficult, but this cannot be an excuse.

I have made progress in smiling more when leading or speaking to groups. And it works. It sets the tone for the meeting and improves the audience's mood. So, SMILE MORE!

I DO APPRECIATE YOU, AND I HOPE YOU APPRECIATE THIS

OUR WORLD

All the time, maybe even every day, we encounter people in our lives who, even in the smallest of ways, help us along in our journey. And every one of them has faults because they are human. Some of them are even irritating.

We take these people for granted. We expect them to help, assist, serve, listen to us, whatever. It just becomes routine. We don't notice that they work hard and are struggling with personal issues (just like us, right?). They just fade into the background of our lives until we don't notice them at all, like bit players in a story where we are the main character.

Until they are gone, sometimes forever, and we miss them. Maybe only then do we realize their worth to us.

Therefore, we need to tell everyone in our lives that we *appreciate* them when they do something to help us.

This goes one step beyond an obligatory "thank you". True appreciation sounds like this:

"Thanks for doing this for me. I really <u>appreciate</u> your help."

Or maybe just: "I really <u>appreciate</u> you."

Regardless, one word we all need to say more is "appreciate".

Appreciate, appreciate, appreciate, appreciate.

Because people want to feel appreciated. People need to feel appreciated. So please, tell them you appreciate them.

And I'm not just talking about your close friends and main squeeze. No, you need to tell even the people you don't particularly like—even those irritating people with those irritating faults—that you appreciate their effort and contributions.

Everyone brings something to the party. Make sure they are recognized for it.

We all need to know we are significant to someone for something. There are many people around me whom I expect things from. I expect, I expect, I expect, and I can get cranky when these expectations are not met on time or even at all. However, I need to appreciate it more when these expectations are achieved, and especially when they are exceeded.

Recently, I said farewell to a friend who was moving far away. This person had done a tremendous job on an important project for me. And yes, I said my obligatory "thank you," but the last time I saw them in person, I failed to say how much I appreciated the effort. I did realize my omission later that evening and expressed my appreciation in an email. But those words needed to be said in person, and yet somehow, they failed to leave my lips. I don't say those words enough and have tried to be much more appreciative lately.

A few weeks ago, a high school friend died of cancer. I was touched by the comments my classmates posted on Facebook. Yes, everyone says good things about the recently departed, but these praises were plentiful, and more importantly, they were genuine. Some who hadn't seen the man in years were appreciative of the life he had lived, the person he was. I know the guy would have been totally astonished if he could have read all the tributes listed there (Who knows? Maybe he could...). My classmates didn't have the opportunity to express their appreciation in person because few had had contact with him recently. So, I hope that the people in his world had told him in person some of the same things that were posted on Facebook after his passing:

that they appreciated him, the work that he did, and the life that he led.

Thus the need, decency, and urgency to tell those in our world that we appreciate them. Because these are things you need to tell them in person, and you never know when it will be too late to do so.

And so, even though I may never meet most of you in person, I appreciate you for reading this. I appreciate all of you who have bought my books, read my blogs, offered words of encouragement, and are on my team. Your support is so important to me, more than you will ever know. And if you are a friend or associate in my own world, I appreciate you, too.

And I would greatly appreciate it if you heed these words. Peace.

BE KIND

This essay was written in late February 2020, just before the pandemic changed our world. As the virus spread, we became fearful and therefore harsher with our fellow man. We hoarded toilet paper and screamed at those who responded to the circumstances differently than we did.

These words could not have come at a more appropriate time.

Because someone, somewhere needs to hear this ...

I made a 2020 New Year's resolution to be kind or be kind*er*.

"Aww, Don, that is so great of you! You are such an awesome person. You want to be kind to people. You are so wonderful ..."

No, not so much. For me to have to make this resolution means that I have *not* been kind to people recently.

I have been mean. I have been inconsiderate. I have been a jerk. So much so that I am aware I need to change my behavior. Thus, the resolution.

My rude behavior became an issue at the start of 2018. That year began with a horrible case of influenza, followed closely by the death of my dog. Then, there was a series of frustrating problems with the release of my second book. By March, I was totally fizzed off at the world. So much so that I aggressively unloaded on two people on the phone who had done nothing wrong (one was even work-related).

My mood, and thus my behavior, didn't improve much that year. And I continued to be highly cranky in 2019, as I struggled with health issues for most of the year.

I'd like to think these are valid reasons for my bad behavior. But often, my "reasons" are really just excuses.

In reality, I have been *irritated* for two years and have responded by being *irritating* to others.

Let's think through this logic:

I'm irritated, so I will make other people irritated, too.

I'm angry, so I will make other people angry, too.

I'm frustrated...

This behavior is like that of a third-grader. It is easy to see when others are irritating, but not so apparent when we ourselves are the agitators.

So, I decided to make this resolution to be kind or kind*er* this year. I expected this resolution to be easy because I'm not *actually* rude that often, am I?

Yes, it's a New Year's resolution, but I got this!

(Insert hysterical laughter here).

However, my work year hadn't even begun when I got an email from a colleague totally ignoring the agreed-to plan for dealing with an important project the first week of January. That fizzed me off, and I immediately started to construct a snarky email scolding him for not following my plan.

Then, I remembered: Be Kind.

I ignored their indiscretion and proceeded with things that week as initially planned. And guess what? Even though I wasn't snarky, everything turned out great.

But this was going to be much more difficult than I thought, so I posted a small "Be Kind" sign on the wall above my desk to remind me of my resolution. And I needed that help because the following week, a coworker messaged me a stupid question right in the middle of a hectic day. I had already answered this question *just* an hour before, and now I had to take the time to repeat myself. Once again, I began to type a cynical email.

But then I remembered: This coworker is dealing with a serious health condition. They probably shouldn't even be working. So, I simply answered their question again with no disparaging comments.

"Don, you are such an angel! Being so nice and kind to that sick coworker. I wish I were as wonderful as you..."

And then it hit me:

WHAT DIFFERENCE DOES IT MAKE?

Why should it matter at all if the coworker has cancer or some other serious disease? Should I be kind only to the sick and dying? Why wouldn't I be just as kind to the healthy and living? It should not make any difference at all.

And just when I thought I was making excellent progress, disaster struck on February 10th.

Usually, you break your resolutions without much fanfare. Maybe you slip up a little here, a little there, until you just give up and gradually return to your old habits. In many cases, you even forget your resolution by the end of January. But the "Be Kind" sign was beneficial to helping me remember.

But not this year. I didn't just break my resolution—I *pulverized* it into little pieces that exploded all over me and anyone else in the area. This happened away from the house, out of sight from that sign on the wall, the one that had been so helpful.

I won't say what I did because I have a bad temper and it was embarrassing. But rest assured, it was unkind. It was extremely unkind, third-grader-type behavior that an apology won't undo.

Typically, when you break a resolution, you say, "Oh, well. At least I tried," and go on with life, even if it's January 2nd. But maybe this kindness resolution requires more effort. Maybe it deserves a second chance.

And kind people are my favorite type of people. The best people I have ever known have also been the most kind. They make you feel good, and those are the people you like to be around. When someone extends kindness to you, it makes you feel special.

Want to be more popular? Be kind.

Want people to treat you better? Be kind.

Want to attract a lover? Don't concentrate on being sexy. Be kind.

Showing kindness is too important to dismiss. Our society is becoming ruder and less kind every day. Our politicians and corporate gods are unkind. Our celebrities and tweeters are unkind. There is a kindness shortage. There is a kindness crisis. Therefore, kindness is a valuable commodity that we desperately need more of.

We can't change the world tomorrow, but I assure you we can change *our* world tomorrow—just by being kind to everyone we encounter. Yes, that's some deep, heavy stuff right there.

THE BOOK mentions "kind" or "kindness" over 80 times. It doesn't command us to be kind as much as it reminds us of how good kindness is. It assumes we already *know* we should be kind, so it encourages us to do what we already know we should.

And I know I should be kinder, that I should extend kindness to others whether they deserve it or not. Whether they are sick or not. Whether they are weak or not. Even if I don't like them, I need to be kind to them.

So, the resolution may have been broken, but the sign stays on the wall. And the journey continues...

REACT OR RESPOND? THERE IS A VAST DIFFERENCE.

Your boss, spouse, coworker, colleague, child, acquaintance, a stranger, or sometimes even a friend unexpectedly unleashes a verbal tirade upon you. Perhaps it's just a casual statement that highly annoys you.

You feel (pick as many as you want): angered, threatened, demeaned, disrespected, marginalized, insulted, offended, disgusted, fearful, irritated, or repulsed.

So, how do you react? Or, more importantly: How do you respond?

"Don, that question is redundant, isn't it? 'React' and 'respond' are the same thing, right?"

No, they are not. And understanding the difference can change your life.

"Are you telling me that knowing the distinction between these two similar words is that important? How?"

When you *react* to people, it is an emotional outburst most likely delivered with the same antagonism as the offending statement. You speak without thinking; the words fire out of your mouth like a submachine gun. The speech is angry, sarcastic, caustic, venomous, biting, cutting, and hurtful.

"Reactions" can destroy relationships and reputations. Reactions can produce hurt feelings and pain that sometimes take years to heal. Reactions cost people their marriages, jobs, friends, and sometimes even their lives.

Reactions almost always lead to arguments rather than discussions. Unfortunately, these arguments lead to even more reactions, with both parties' verbal weapons blasting away. If you need examples, just look at the "flame wars" on Facebook, Twitter, and other sites.

"Well, yes, reactions are bad, but why are responses any different?"

A *response* is a rational, calmer action designed to diffuse the situation and start a discussion instead of a heated argument. An essential aspect of a "response" is to gain insight into *why* the person has just unloaded upon you. Therefore, one of the best responses starts with you asking a question. If you can't think of a question related to the subject, a good place to start is: *Why are you so upset?*

This allows you to better understand the situation, enables the other person to either continue to vent or calm down, and gives you time to formulate a second, more relevant question. Sometimes, asking "Why are you so upset?" will totally change the tenor of the discussion, as the person realizes they might have spoken too forcibly. Often, they will apologize, and then a purposeful conversation can begin.

"But Don, how does letting the other person keep ranting and raving help things?"

Because it puts you in control of the situation. While the other person is out of control, you can formulate your response. You may choose to disagree, but it is possible to do so in a calm, mature manner. You may even decide to be charming in your reply. But the goal is to defuse the situation, not escalate it.

Unfortunately, your calm response may sometimes enrage the person even more because they are simply looking for a fight, not an intelligent discussion. But even then, you can remain in control and respond accordingly. Just because they want a fight doesn't mean you must participate.

There are situations in which you will have time before you must choose to "respond" or "react". For example, when you get upset by an email, Facebook post, or tweet. How often have you reacted to that situation with an emotionally charged, nasty tirade? How did that work out for you? It made you feel good in the moment, but it caused you to regret it for much longer. When you have time to formulate a response, the critical question is: *What do I want to happen next?*

Once you know what the desirable outcome of the situation is, craft a careful, strategic response that supports your intent. Resist the temptation to say to yourself: *"I'm going to give him a piece of my mind!"*; *"I'm going to show her just how stupid she is!"*; *"I'm going to show them who's boss!"*; etc.

These reactions make us feel good in the moment, but if after the smoke clears, the situation hasn't changed—or maybe it has gotten worse—what have you gained? You still wake up tomorrow with an ongoing conflict or problem.

Look! There's a raging conflict burning out of control. Is it better to pour gasoline on it (a reaction)? Or is it better to pour water on it (a response)? You very rarely must apologize for a response, but you often must apologize for a reaction.

"Okay, Don, reactions are harmful. But they are just natural tendencies. It's what I do in that situation. It's what I've always done. How do I change that?"

And now, we come to the difficult part of this post. Easy to say, hard to do.

Like with many of the good new habits from this chapter, the best way to start doing it is to *start doing it.*

Next time someone sends you an angry email? Respond instead of reacting. Next time someone tweets at you trying to start a fight? Respond instead of reacting. Next time you get into a heated argument with your friend? Respond instead of reacting.

Remind yourself to do it. And then do it.

This is a learned behavior, but the sooner you understand and can implement this change, the better your life will be. Again, it can improve your marriage, relationships, career, etc. It is one of the most valuable life skills to acquire and practice.

So, the next time you are faced with a conflict, will you react, or will you respond?

WE COULD USE A SHOT OF EMPATHY RIGHT NOW

They are seemingly everywhere: The woman with the pronounced limp. The man moving slowly, leaning on his cane. The person arduously straining, climbing one step at a time. And it's just not the elderly—the people having difficulty walking come in all ages. Call them the "mobility-challenged" individuals.

But you don't notice them. They are invisible to you. They blend into the background. However, you are highly aware of them when they happen to impede your progress. When they slow you down. It can be incredibly frustrating if you are behind the slow-moving person climbing the stairs or approaching a single-door entrance or exit.

And that was my view of the "mobility-challenged" until last year, when I suffered a gout attack that caused my right ankle to swell enormously. I was house-ridden for a couple of weeks, and the pain was so intense it was difficult to even move around the house.

Eventually, I was able to drive my car and venture out with the help of my cane. And that's when I became aware of every "mobility-challenged" person I witnessed. My pain had made me sensitive to a group of people who had always been there but I'd never seen. Instinctively, I would ask myself:

What ailment is causing her problem?

Is he in great pain?

Will she get any better–or worse?

Is this a permanent or temporary condition? (Especially if the person is young)

My situation had made me highly sensitive to the struggles, discomfort, and pain of others. Now, it wasn't "those people"—it was *us* because I was one of "those people". I had been given a hefty dose of what we call "empathy".

Webster's defines empathy as: *"The action of understanding, being aware of, being sensitive to, and vicariously experiencing the feelings, thoughts, and experience of another."*

And empathy is what is needed most right now in our chaotic environment. The action of being able to understand the feelings, thoughts, and experiences of others. Of others much different than us. Of others who think different. Of others who look different. Of others who see life different and have had different life experiences. Of others whose possessions are more or less than what we have.

Some forces are trying to divide us politically, racially, by economic class, etc. It's all division, and it's all harmful. But empathy, by definition, unites us. It creates a shared understanding. I am willing to make an effort to understand you. You are making an effort to understand me. It is at this point when the yelling, name-calling, arguing, and rioting stops. It is where the essential discussion begins.

We cannot solve any of these serious problems without empathy.

And the empathy must be shared by *all*. If you expect me to empathize with you, you must be willing to extend the same empathy to me. This means we may fundamentally disagree on many issues, but we still understand each other's feelings, thoughts, and experiences. This is not a one-way street but a circular discussion that creates *unity*.

Being empathetic takes effort. My ankle is now completely healed, although it could flare up again at any time. I am now patient when "inconvenienced" by the mobility-challenged; however, I am not as *empathetic* because my own pain is gone.

THE BOOK tells us to: *"Rejoice with those who rejoice, weep with those who weep."** The rejoicing part is fun and easy. The weeping is much more difficult.

Empathy means I will not judge. I will not shout. I will not become angry or bitter. I will seek to understand. I will seek solutions to the problems. I will seek peace.

How Empathy Works in Real Life

Nancy and I grew up in nearby neighborhoods during the same era. We graduated the same year from the same high school. Since then, we have both attained success in our careers, becoming respected professionals—not a small achievement, considering our middle-class, blue-collar roots. We are two highly intelligent professionals with seemingly very similar backgrounds.

So, we should hold matching political views, correct? No, not even close. We happen to be on different sides of the political spectrum.

How is this possible? Nancy's situation in her home growing up was very different than mine. Her childhood experiences instilled in her many emotions, concepts, and feelings that were different from mine. They gave her a different perspective and imparted deep empathy for people currently in the same situation as she once endured.

Nancy and I were friends but lost touch after high school. However, we now see each other occasionally at high school class get-togethers, and when we do, in addition to catching up on life, we discuss politics.

"What?! WHAT?!?!?! Why would you ever do that?!?!?!?!?! Are you insane?!?!?!?!?!?!?!?!?! You guys disagree on everything! You should never talk about politics!"

No, these talks are not what you would expect in these hyper-partisan times. They are civil. No one shouts. No one even raises their voice. There are as many smiles as there are frowns. Each person calmly expresses a thought while the other listens actively and intently, never anticipating an opportunity to pounce and interrupt, having discovered a contradiction in the other's "flawed" views.

The conversations are honest. We both feel safe expressing what we genuinely believe without fear of judgment or condemnation. Nancy even has this habit of grinning like an ornery ten-year-old right before saying something she knows will elicit a response. And this is fine because it is difficult to get angry when a person is smiling at you.

Nancy is my friend, and she trusts me. And I trust her, which leads to a more in-depth conversation.

The discussions are also at a very high level. These are two wise, intelligent, well-informed people discussing deep, heavy stuff. There are no talking points, no cliches, but there are admissions of problems with both political parties and changes that need to happen.

The unexpected result of these discussions is that Nancy and I agree on much more than we disagree. The main differences exist in our views of *how* to solve the problems we face. If more people could have these types of discussions, our nation would be better off, and some major, persistent problems just might (gasp) actually get solved.

But this "magic" doesn't happen without empathy. I understand why Nancy believes what she does, and she knows where I'm coming from as well. This realization allows us to have a *discussion* and not a *debate*. With these talks, I'm not trying to change who she is. Nancy is a beautiful person and a great friend. She is the sum of her life experiences—such as I am, and such as we all are. My empathy allows me to value her and her opinions as she respects mine. I feel positive at the end of our talks, instead of angry and exasperated as I might be after discussing these same topics with most people these days.

The term "finding common ground" is thrown around a lot. It is much easier to locate that "common ground" when you understand, are aware of, and are sensitive to the other person—or "side", as it may be.

Discussing complex issues with Nancy gives me new insights into these issues. New concepts to ponder. New ideas to consider. A perspective I would not possess if I didn't risk having a deep, meaningful conversation with a friend whose views are much different than mine. But it only works with *empathy*. And that's why we need more of it in our lives.

Empathy: *"The action of understanding, being aware of, being sensitive to, and vicariously experiencing the feelings, thoughts, and experience of another."* (Webster's)

'* Romans 12:15

CHAPTER 12: LIFE LESSONS

This final chapter includes deep, heavy stuff that didn't fit well within the subjects of the preceding chapters. But just like people who have difficulties fitting in, these essays still have value!

WERE YOU REALLY A BAD PARENT?

I hear this all the time:

"Don, I was a bad parent because I made so many mistakes."

Well, you are a better parent than you think.

The fact that you still fret over this and are concerned about your children, no matter their age, means you cared about your kids then, and you still care about them now.

That alone makes you a good parent.

But what about those bad decisions?

Well, in most situations in life, we accept the fact that we'll make mistakes, that we're not perfect. However, we still expect to be perfect parents—to be flawless in our choices. To have the superhuman power to know and control the outcome of every decision we make regarding our children.

But you are not a perfect person, so stop believing you should be a perfect parent. You aren't. No one is.

But you are a better parent than you think. You have made many more good decisions than bad ones regarding your children. The problem is, like in all areas of life, we remember all the wrong choices we made because of the consequences that occurred. And we never expected, nor wanted, those harmful, hurtful outcomes. We don't remember the right choices we made for our kids because they produced the good outcomes we were hoping for and expected. Those excellent decisions tend to get erased from our memory, even though they greatly benefitted our children.

Some of those "bad" decisions you made weren't even poor decisions. They were good decisions that resulted in adverse outcomes. You make the best decisions you can at the time with the best information you have. But you are not all-knowing. You are not perfect. However, if you make the choices that you believe will benefit your kid, you are a good parent.

Of course, there are those tough decisions where there is no good alternative—choosing the lesser of two evils. Again, you tend to remember the bad outcome (which is almost assured in this situation), but you forget that it was a difficult decision to begin with and you made what you considered the best choice available.

If you care about your children, if you love your children enough to try to make the best decisions you can for them, then you are a good parent. You are not going to make all the right choices. You are not—and were never going to be—the *perfect* parent.

Therefore: STOP SECOND-GUESSING EVERY CHOICE YOU MADE AS A PARENT! IF YOU DID THE BEST YOU COULD UNDER THE CIRCUMSTANCES, YOU WERE A GOOD PARENT. You might have even been a great parent.

And it's harmful to beat yourself up over decisions made in the past on things you cannot change. It's much better to focus your attention on the choices you are making now, which impact the things you can change.

EVEN IF YOUR DECISIONS WERE GOOD ...

"But Don, my children didn't turn out as planned."

Well, of course not. Because they seldom do. You planned for great things and may only have received good things. Please be satisfied with that.

And if the outcomes were not good? It is not *your* fault.

Parenting is one of the toughest challenges there is because the outcome is so highly uncertain. Parenting is even more complicated than those mathematical equations it takes geniuses months to solve.

The parenting calculation takes at least eighteen years to finish, and the equation frequently changes over time. Just about the time you master how to parent a pre-teen—BOOM! You must parent a teenager, and your math problem just turned from algebra to calculus.

But you can't really "solve" this problem, can you? You can put all the right numbers in, do all the right things, and still not get the desired result.

Because your job is not to ensure your child's success in life—it is to prepare your child to have the *opportunity* for success in life. Because at some point, your children will make their own decisions, which are typically different than yours. And they must live with their own outcomes.

The choices your children make do not reflect poorly on you, especially if they contradict everything you tried to teach them. If things in your adult children's lives take a terrible turn, you have not failed as a parent; many times, your children just make poor decisions. And again, sometimes they were the right decisions that had bad outcomes.

I have several friends who are great people and were great parents. However, they had children who made extremely poor choices after they became adults. These children even became estranged from these excellent parents for a period, for no logical reason at all. A close friend's daughter died of an opioid overdose in her 20's. Another friend's son committed suicide. Were they bad parents? No, these are good people, and they were all excellent parents, and *none of these outcomes are their fault.*

You can do everything—well, almost everything—right and still not have things turn out well. You can provide as much training as possible for your children to make good choices, but you can't make those choices for them. Your adult child's success, or lack thereof, is not a reflection of you.

And good parents will want to continue to parent their adult children because, of course, they are good parents, and they care about the welfare of their kids no matter their age. But you must resist this temptation. We must at some point, stop parenting and just start advising. Because it is their choice where to work, where to live, how to raise their own kids, etc. Their decisions, not yours. (Mothers-in-law, I'm talking to you!)

So: STOP BLAMING YOURSELF FOR THE CHOICES YOUR ADULT CHILDREN MAKE! IT IS THEIR CHOICE, NOT YOURS. SO, STOP IT! STOP IT NOW!

You are a better parent than you think. And if you cared about your children and tried to provide for and train them as best you could, you were/are a good parent.

YOU HAVE NO IDEA WHAT THESE PARENTS FACE

We just discussed parenting and how difficult that task is with all the variables, tough choices, etc. But now, let's raise the bar... turn it up a notch. While we're at it, let's just turn the dial all the way to the right.

Parenting healthy kids is challenging, but what about parenting children with "irregular needs"? (I'm not using the term "special needs" because I want this to include any and every type of ongoing physical, mental, and personality disorder—all of them. Throw in alcohol, drug, and whatever addictions, too).

How difficult is it to parent a child with irregular needs?

You have no idea. Trust me. You have no idea. I only have some idea because my daughter's cerebral palsy is considered relatively mild. Of course, people whose children are only moderately impacted tend to minimize their situation when talking about it. Like my friend Marc, who was quick to point out that his autistic son is "higher functioning" whenever we discuss our parenting challenges. But if your kid has any abnormality, any issue, any challenge, or any other "irregular need", your task as a parent becomes exponentially more difficult.

Take those problematic parental decisions, for example. When dealing with an "irregular-needs" child, sometimes you are facing ten possible outcomes, instead of just two, and nine of those outcomes may be bad. Often, you must make these critical decisions with little or even inaccurate information. And then those bad decisions (again, not necessarily poor decisions, just choices that lead to adverse outcomes, often beyond your control) cause you to have to make even more decisions. Then, there are choices so complicated, the best you can do is just guess.

When things go wrong—which sometimes is a daily occurrence—you blame yourself, and you and your spouse must deal with the consequences. You second-guess yourself a lot. You second-guess your spouse. You triple-guess yourself. Some days, you "guess" yourself repeatedly and conclude you are an idiot and a sad excuse for a parent.

This second-guessing and these repeated setbacks, both of which are inevitable, put incredible stress on relationships. My friend Marc states, "Nobody can imagine the strain on a marriage during these incredibly difficult times." Many marriages do not survive the pressure of raising an irregular-needs child. In most of these cases, the husband bails due to the overwhelming stress. Even though I do not condone this action, I also cannot judge people who are under this much pressure. At times, the enormous amount of stress is crushing.

Besides the typical responsibilities, parents of irregular-needs kids play many roles. You must be a doctor, therapist, psychologist, and priest, all at the same time. It requires superhuman knowledge, superhuman strength, superhuman patience, and superhuman compassion. Parents of irregular-needs children are as close to real superheroes as you are ever going to get.

For example, I have a friend who adopted a baby who has cerebral palsy. Only she didn't know the girl's condition at the time of the adoption. They hid it from her. They basically stuck her with this child. I would have been extremely bitter and tried to get out of the deal. My friend's reaction, however? She has made it her life's mission to raise this kid in an exemplary manner. She has poured her life into that girl. That's superhuman love.

Another friend is raising three autistic sons. That's right—after having two sons with autism, he had another boy who has the same condition. And now, he has a great family, which he loves tremendously. His wife runs a support group for parents of irregular-needs kids. That's superhuman strength and then some.

And these parents are everywhere. Over the past few years, I have learned that several of my associates are captaining the same boat. I have learned about the children of my good friend Dave, my long-time friend Mike, my accountant Tim, the man mentioned in the previous paragraph, and the daughter of a coworker. Yes, irregular-needs children are much more common than you realize, and I'm sure you have a friend or family member in the same position as these people here.

Having an irregular-needs child impacts every family decision you make. I was downsized from my job just after my daughter's seventh birthday. I didn't care that I lost that job. I didn't care about the impact to my career. I wasn't very concerned about not having money to pay the everyday bills. But what mattered most was that I had lost my medical insurance, which had put the welfare of my daughter at risk. I drove an hour to an important interview in a negative 20-degree wind chill, having a fever of over 102 degrees, to get the job that would restore that insurance. You just do whatever it takes—repeatedly.

Oh, and those decisions. My wife and I decided to send my daughter away to college in Indiana. I knew there were risks involved, but I thought it would help my daughter's social development. Leaving the campus after dropping her off was one of the most gut-wrenching days of my entire life.

It was the correct decision, but it was almost the worst decision I have ever made. There was an incident, a dangerous accident that nearly cost my daughter her life. Of course, I wasn't there to witness it, but it was all right there in the extensive police report. And then I had to make another decision about whether to drive to Indiana and pull her out of school. I decided to let her stay—again, the correct choice. However, if she would have died there, I would have never forgiven myself.

Yeah, that's what it's like. A bunch of difficult choices in a game you might—if you're lucky—be able to play well, but you can never win.

But you can't see the tremendous stress on these parents from the outside looking in. You might think, *"Becky's daughter has Down Syndrome, but she handles it so well!"*

But the truth is, it's heavy. It's massive. It's burdensome. And it's persistent. You have no idea. That person you know with the irregular-needs child—please cut them some slack. Show them some compassion. Tell them they are appreciated. Because you have no idea what your friend or coworker parenting their irregular-needs child has had to deal with that morning, nor the perilous situation they know is waiting for them at home that evening. You have no idea...

If a person is parenting an irregular-needs child, then they have irregular needs themselves. Please extend them grace accordingly.

Two Wrongs Don't Make a Right

"Two wrongs don't make a right."

That's some of the best advice my father ever gave me. I heard it every time someone had wronged me and I verbalized how I planned to get revenge.

My father never told me not to take the action. He didn't ask me the details of the situation. There was no discussion of my feelings or the consequences of my strategic mischief.

No, it was just six simple words. The first time he said it, I was confused. I had to think it through, but even as a young boy, I got the message: What I was about to do was wrong, and it would not correct the offense done to me. I always had no response to his proclamation—not a word. You can't dispute this idiom. Two wrongs never make a right. You may as well try to argue that one plus one does not equal two.

But I heard these words from my father often—I guess I liked to tell him about my misguided plans—and every time, I disliked hearing this expression because I knew it was true and I would not be seeking revenge. And I heard it enough that it is permanently burned in my brain. Unfortunately, I have not always followed this principle. But that's because I'm not a saint, not because it isn't valid.

If you don't believe the concept is genuine, then let me refer you to THE BOOK, which puts it this way:

If someone has done you wrong, do not repay him with a wrong.*

Or, if you prefer:

Do not repay anyone evil for evil.*

But I still prefer my father's simple version:

"Two wrongs don't make a right."

And right now, we need to trust these six words more than ever. We, as a people, have sailed far off course and need desperately to right our ship. Our culture now views revenge as acceptable if it is done for the right reason—in other words, we are encouraged to become social vigilantes.

Example: This person was killed unjustly. Therefore, our response is to create terror.

Believe it or not, many people perpetuating the problem do believe "two wrongs don't make a right." However, their response is not to do the right things—it's to keep doing additional wrong things. Yes, *two* wrongs don't make a right, so we'll do *three* wrongs, fifty wrongs, and two hundred wrongs to try to make it right, balance things out, and thus create a perverse type of justice. The antagonists will even use past wrongs to justify all their current wrongs, while still believing their actions are pure and noble.

But if one wrong done in response to something is, in fact, wrong, then continued wrongs just make the situation worse—much, much worse. No matter how many wrongs you commit, you don't make it right. You are just more wrong.

And referring back to THE BOOK, if you keep repaying evil for evil, you generate a tremendous amount of evil. A society filled with evil is a dangerous place. And as these events unfold before us in real time, you can feel the presence of evil among us. All because…

"Two wrongs don't make a right."

This doesn't absolve us from addressing some past wrongs. But it is nearly impossible to have meaningful dialogues that lead to constructive change when so much evil payback is occurring.

But the proverb applies to everyone, every time. We will destroy ourselves when there is an initial wrong, which is responded to with another wrong, which is in turn responded to with yet another wrong, until there is an endless feedback loop of wrongs which, all put together, will never result in a right. Nothing is being accomplished. No problems are being resolved. The only result is more hatred and more evil. That's why THE BOOK warns against repaying evil for evil. And my father's wisdom is still golden:

"Two wrongs don't make a right."

WE ARE ALL PILGRIMS THIS YEAR

Context: This essay was written in November 2021, as another (hopefully the last) big wave of the virus was raging in the country.

This essay is about the plague, the virus, the scourge— the pandemic, if you will.

Wait, don't go! It's different than the thousands of commentaries already written on this subject.

You see, I don't care if you wear a mask, don't wear a mask, if you're vaccinated, non-vaccinated, if you're a virus survivor, skeptic, Democrat, Republican, Independent, or something else entirely.

I do care that when you inhale, your lungs fill with air. If they do, you are still alive. This means you have survived the scourge so far. This is no small accomplishment. I have told people over the past two years, "If you celebrate a birthday during a pandemic, it is a blessed occasion. If you celebrate two, even better."

You see, 765,000 Americans have died from the virus.

Oh, you want to argue that the number is too *high* because deaths for other illnesses were intentionally misclassified to blow the whole thing out of proportion because of something called "Big Pharma"? Okay...

Oh, you want to argue that the number is too *low* because many people died without ever making it to a testing site or hospital so they can't technically be counted as "virus" deaths? Okay...

Since I'm a numbers guy, let's just assume these two extremes totally cancel each other out, and 765,000 (and counting) is a reasonable average estimate. The count worldwide is at 5.1 million (again, an average estimate).

And this is because pandemics kill people. That's what pandemics do. We hadn't had a severe pandemic since 1918. The frustrating part is that even though mankind is 100 years smarter and even though medical technology has advanced exponentially, we still can't keep a lethal microbe from killing us. Mask on, mask off, shots, jabs, distancing, quarantines—it's still striking us dead.

But even though it's killed 765,000 of your countrymen, it hasn't gotten *you*. You have not been infected. Or you were infected, but your immune system neutralized it. Or you became ill (I'm in this category), and you were able to survive.

Which brings us to Thanksgiving. These days, we really don't give much thanks. We take our wealth, health, and blessings so much for granted. Maybe on Thursday, we say a group prayer before we gluttonously gorge ourselves on the holiday feast. But that's about it.

The Pilgrims started all this, and if you read the history, you will find that they were essentially thanking THE CREATOR that they were still alive on that first Thanksgiving. That is a strange concept when you think about it. But the Pilgrims had that "faith" thing down right, much more than our present culture. So, we find ourselves back to the beginning, so to speak. Back to the basics. Back to "life-or-death".

This has been a brutal year. Besides the fatal virus, add in the cancers, the accidents, the illnesses, the overdoses, plus everything else, and it becomes very likely that death has claimed someone in your circle during 2021. (My posse has been hit hard this year.)

So, after making it through this dreadful year and still being able to draw breath through our lungs, we, like the Pilgrims, need to offer up thanks to THE CREATOR for our life—our *actual* life. For still being alive, when so many others have perished.

And I'm not talking about just "being thankful" or "feeling thankful" or "making a list of things to be thankful for". No, not enough. Not even close. There is a difference between feeling wealthy and actually *being* wealthy. There is a difference between feeling blessed and actually *being* blessed. So, there is an enormous difference between feeling thankful and actually *giving* thanks.

The Pilgrims got it. They really got it. That's why the holiday is called *Thanks*giving. So today, it's time to literally get on your knees and give thanks to THE CREATOR for continuing to give you life (Yes, I am going to do this as well). This giving of thanks will provide a spiritual cleansing. This is greatly needed since the virus has infected more than our bodies—it has infected our souls. And there is no vaccine to fix that.

I give thanks to THE CREATOR for your life...

REMEMBER THIS, MY FRIEND...

We have come to the end of all the deep, heavy stuff to discuss for now.

But remember these truths, my friend...

- Be generous to others in need.
- Give, and it will be given back to you in ways you do not expect.
- Do acts of kindness—but with a purpose.
- See the need—meet the need.
- Carry an extra $20 around so you can meet spontaneous needs.
- Do not let circumstances and culture steal your Christmas joy.
- Do not allow materialism to ruin your Christmas.
- Say "Merry Christmas" because you are indeed talking about Christmas.
- Share your blessings with the less fortunate, especially at Christmas.
- Traumatic events will shape your life forever. You may need the help of others to recover.
- When tragedy strikes, don't ask "Why me?"— accept that you now must deal with it in the best way possible.
- Sometimes, a little hope and lots of prayer lead to good results.
- You must deal with what life gives you. Concentrate on making it the best life you can.
- Find joy in the simple things in life. Don't put so much pressure on yourself that you don't have fun.

- Don't let others determine whether you are good enough to achieve your goals. Give it your best shot and then decide for yourself.
- You may not be good enough...yet.
- Sometimes, you must raise your game to overcome the obstacles in your life.
- Believing that your employer is loyal to you is the adult equivalent of believing in Santa Claus.
- Sometimes, teachers/bosses are helping you by being tough on you.
- Mentors can see talents you don't realize you possess. Listen to them.
- Be a mentor to anyone who needs your guidance.
- Be generous with your kind words—they can have a big impact you will never see.
- People can help you in ways you disagree with.
- No one is perfect—so stop expecting them to be.
- If you see someone who needs a friend, befriend them.
- Realize that everyone who you think is your friend is not actually your friend.
- Be there when your friends are in distress—it could save their lives.
- Help your friends reach their full potential by encouraging them to pursue their dreams.
- At times in life, you will hit bottom—climbing out of that pit is worth it.
- Help other people recover if they hit bottom.
- Things get better over time.
- It's not what you lost that is ultimately important—it's what you still have.
- You are not a loser—either you believe in yourself, or you don't.

- Resilience, Persistence, and Perseverance are the keys to overcoming obstacles.
- You can fail repeatedly and still win the war, as long as you don't stop fighting.
- Weak prayers can get answered—if they are honest ones.
- Help your friends in this life—they won't be here forever.
- Our longtime friends can change due to physical and mental issues we don't see. We need to cut them some slack.
- Appreciate the great people who cross your path. Try to emulate them.
- Cherish your great friendships because they can end suddenly.
- Seek to figure out this after-death question now, while you still have time.
- Be careful what you say to people who are grieving.
- Invite grieving people out for coffee and let them express their feelings.
- The sorrow felt from the death of a dog or other beloved pet can be as strong as a loss of a person.
- We are faithful creatures—everyone has faith in something.
- Be very careful where you place your faith.
- Religion is a poor substitute for actual faith.
- Sometimes, the worst tragedies in life lead to good things later.
- A small amount of pure faith is a powerful element.
- Hate destroys you from within—so don't be a hater.

- Be the person who decreases the amount of hate in your world.
- Make peace with your nemesis, and good things will happen.
- Forgiveness is a process that benefits you, not necessarily the other person.
- Say "please" and "thank you" at every opportunity.
- Smile more.
- Appreciate all the people in your life, even the "minor" ones.
- Be kind and show kindness—our world desperately needs this right now.
- Respond to difficult situations—don't react to them.
- Show empathy to people—you never know what struggles they're facing.
- Learn by having honest discussions with people who look at the world differently than you.
- You are/were a better parent than you think.
- Parents of special/irregular-needs kids are superheroes
- Two wrongs don't make a right.
- If you are still alive after the first major pandemic in 100 years, give thanks!

'*Romans 12:17